ALTERNATIVES TO COGNITION
A New Look at Explaining
Human Social Behavior

ALTERNATIVES TO COGNITION
A New Look at Explaining
Human Social Behavior

Christina Lee
University of Newcastle

LEA LAWRENCE ERLBAUM ASSOCIATES, PUBLISHERS

1998 Mahwah, New Jersey   London

Lawrence Erlbaum Associates
10 Industrial Avenue
Mahwah, NJ 07430

Library of Congress Cataloging-in-Publication Data

Lee, Christina
    Alternatives to cognition : a new look at explaining
human social behavior / Christina Lee.
        p. cm.
    Includes bibliographical references and index.
    ISBN 0-8058-2654-8 (alk. paper)
    1. Cognitive psychology. 2. Psychology—Philosophy.
I. Title.
BF201.L44 1997
153—dc21   97-12615
                                                   CIP

Printed in the United States of America
10 9 8 7 6 5 4 3 2 1

Contents

Preface

This volume arose out of a frustration with contemporary psychology, and a belief that a more critical, more flexible approach to the way we understand our subject matter is not only possible but essential if psychology is to realize its potential to become a truly scientific, unsuperstitious, explanation of human behavior in context. Modern psychology's focus on individual cognition, its much heralded "cognitive revolution," reifies cognition and artificially separates it from the person, and the person from the broader physical and social context. The seemingly unchallengeable view that modern psychology is, and should be, the study of individual thought means that biological, social, economic, and environmental realities are ignored. Furthermore, the implicitly dualistic nature of cognitive models, which focus on cognition entirely independently of the real world, militates against an approach that is consistent with modern scientific thought, an approach that views cognition as part of a complex, dynamic physical system. Instead, cognition and, by extension, human behavior, is viewed as something inherently mysterious, unconstrained by the principles that operate in the rest of the universe.

Critical analysis, theoretical analysis based on an awareness of the limitations of any one single worldview, is a minority activity of which the mainstream seems not to approve. Psychology seems to have lost track of the importance of criticism, and to lack a forum within which an open-minded acknowledgment of the potential limitations of any single perspective on our understanding of human beings is seen as a legitimate intellectual activity. Critical psychology has come to be seen as ungenerous and antagonistic, an activity that should be discouraged for its potential to damage our public image and our funding chances, rather than encouraged as the only way in which psychology will progress.

Increasingly, psychological research is theory-confirming research. Variables derived from a single theory are assessed and the relationships between them calculated. It seems easy to forget that psychological models are inventions, not explanations, that psychological theories are plausible but essentially metaphorical inventions, not causal explanations of human behavior.

Furthermore, theoreticians and practitioners alike ignore the political and the philosophical context of our theories. Psychological theories exist in a political context in the broadest sense. Individuals exist in a social, physical, cultural, and historical context, and contemporary theories that ignore context lead, apparently inevitably, to the view that the solutions to human problems must be found in the manipulation of individual cognitions. Within contemporary cognitive psychology, the idea that contextual variables may be maintaining individual distress, that in some cases the best way to help a distressed individual is not to manipulate cognitions but to change aspects of that person's environment, is not one that can even be sensibly entertained.

Theories are also embedded in a philosophical context, in the sense that ideas also exist in the context of metatheories and overarching epistemological positions. The first step in an epistemology of psychological knowledge is an awareness that one has a specific standpoint, one of a range of possible alternatives. Contemporary psychology seems to have lost this awareness, equating currently fashionable modes of thought with some notion of absolute and singular truth.

An exclusive focus on cognition, combined with a reluctance to become aware of the existence of alternative perspectives, is restricting an academic field that has the potential to deal with human behavior in its broadest possible sense: the behavior of individual humans in the context of their biology, their physical and social environment, and their cultural and historical context.

This book does not set out a single alternative to the monolith of cognitive theories; what it tries to do is to develop a more thoughtful, open-minded approach to our subject matter, and to be less dogmatic about the way the world works. I do not expect people to be converted or persuaded by every point in this book, but if I can encourage my colleagues to think a little more seriously about the boundaries of our discipline and about the amount we have to learn from others, then this book will have contributed to the development of a psychology that is at once more rigorous and more relevant to the real world.

ACKNOWLEDGMENTS

The initial proposal for this book was written while I was on sabbatical leave at the Department of Psychology, University of Exeter, England, in 1992, and the final revisions were completed on a subsequent sabbatical leave at the Department of Psychiatry and Behavioural Science, University of Auckland, New Zealand, in 1996. I am grateful to the staff of those two departments, and in particular to Dr. Dick Eiser and Dr. Keith Petrie, for their generosity in providing excellent facilities and ensuring that these academic visits were both productive and enjoyable. I am also grateful to my employer, The University of Newcastle, Australia, which funded both visits.

The majority of the book was researched and written between these two visits, in those vanishingly rare moments in an academic's life between teaching and committee work, student consultations and course administration, marking and justifying one's existence to administration. I am grateful to my colleagues at the Department of Psychology, University of Newcastle, Australia, for their friendship, encouragement, and willingness to humor my wilder notions.

Writing a book is always a solitary activity, and even more so when one takes a stance that is critical of the mainstream within which one works, and it can be difficult to maintain a belief in the value of work of this nature. I am grateful to the journal editors and reviewers who criticized and then accepted the articles that helped to develop these ideas, and I am grateful to those critical psychologists whose writings inspired me and made me feel that I was a small part of a community of scholars.

Most of all, I am grateful to Harry for his patience and his unwavering practical and emotional support.

—Christina Lee

Chapter 1

Cognitive Dominance: The Centrality of Cognitive Explanations in Social Psychology

Modern psychology "admits of no alternative [to cognitive explanations of behavior], since any alternative must be something other than psychology."
—Bolton (1991, p. 104)

Psychology, it is generally acknowledged, has undergone a cognitive revolution (Bootzin, 1985; Sperry, 1993, 1995) in the past decades. Clinical psychology, social psychology, and most of applied psychology are today unquestionably cognitive in outlook. Modern psychology, to a large extent, has no room for noncognitive explanations of behavior. Almost by definition, psychology has become the study of cognition (Bolton, 1991).

Cognitive approaches, we are told, are enjoying overwhelming success in bringing an integrated perspective to the difficult problem of understanding the complexity of human behavior in a suitably scientific manner (e.g., Sperry, 1993, 1995). They have been accepted as an appropriate, adult compromise between the hard-nosed, soulless science of the radical behaviorists on the one hand and the entertaining but fictional models of the psychoanalysts on the other. It appears that academic psychology has passed through its preparadigmatic stage and emerged as a unified, integrated young science. Of course, a healthy level of debate continues, but there is a general agreement on the ground rules. Psychology is the study of individual thought.

The aim of this book is to question the wisdom of this consensus. There are two sides to the question of the role of cognition in human behavior;

one side is currently dominant, but that should not be taken to imply that the other side no longer exists (see, for example, Modgil & Modgil, 1987; Still & Costall, 1991).

This book does not present a single alternative. Rather, I argue that psychology's contemporary emphasis on the cognitive has inhibited the development of alternative approaches to our subject matter. There are theoretical and methodological grounds for rejecting an individualistic, cognition-centered, psychology in favor of the exploration of models that examine interactions between people and with the physical and social environment. Although alternative models may appear undeveloped and lacking the complexity and sophistication of cognitive theories, this may be attributed to current trends in research and scholarship, which favor cognitive approaches, rather than to any fundamental weakness of the models themselves. There is a continuing need to concentrate on what can be established empirically and not to accept points of view simply because they are currently popular and seem to accord with our subjective experiences.

DOMINANCE OF COGNITIVE MODELS

The contemporary dominance of psychology by cognitive-oriented models stands in sharp contrast to the history of the field. Watson (1913), in the paper that effectively founded behaviorism, argued that "psychology as the behaviorist views it is a purely objective experimental branch of natural science" (p. 158). He believed that psychology must restrict itself to the scientific study of observable events and that there was no place in scientific psychology for mind and other nonmaterial concepts. Only events and processes that have material existence, can be measured physically, and can be independently verified, may legitimately be studied. This, of course, meant the development of a psychology that left out the mind, thoughts, dreams, feelings, and subjective experience.

Viewpoints of this type, which emphasised observable behavior, scientific control under laboratory conditions, and the continuities between humans and other animals, dominated psychology for half a century, particularly through the work and influence of Skinner (e.g., Ferster & Skinner, 1957; Skinner, 1953). The past two decades, however, have seen the rise of cognitivism, now arguably the dominant model in psychology. This rise to prominence seems to have come about largely because of dissatisfaction with the perceived limitations on the range of activities that a behaviorist could legitimately study.

It has been argued that a radically behavioral approach must be inadequate to explain the complexity of human experience (Mahoney, 1974; Meichenbaum, 1977; Sperry, 1993). For example, Mahoney (1974) argued that monist materialism (i.e., the view that only the physical world exists) was an inappropriate and overly simplistic philosophical framework for the scientific study of human behavior and that it was impossible for nonmediational models to explain anything so complex as a human being. Beside these arguments, experimental results and clinical techniques that did not seem readily explicable by basic learning principles were appearing. Cognitive mediational explanations were proposed instead, and it was argued that eclectic application of cognitive–behavioral theories was the most effective way for clinical and applied psychology to serve the needs of clients.

Radical behaviorism has today practically disappeared from mainstream psychological journals. Still, a minority of researchers (e.g., Acierno, Hersen, Van Hasselt, & Ammerman, 1994; Eifert, Forsyth, & Schauss, 1993) continue to argue that behavior theory has been misinterpreted and that its rejection is based on a superficial and outdated perception of the field. Although "the limitations of early conditioning models and treatments have led many behavior therapists to abandon conditioning principles and replace them with loosely defined cognitive theories and treatments" (Eifert et al., 1993, p. 107), recent developments in behavior theory could provide a sound scientific basis for a genuine science of psychology (Plaud & Vogeltanz, 1993). The development of behavioral theory and therapy has by no means reached a dead end (Acierno et al., 1994; Eifert & Plaud, 1993; Wyatt, 1990).

However, there is substantial social and professional hostility to behaviorism (Hickey, 1994). Kimble (1989) expressed a widely held view when he argued that a radical science of behavior leaves out "everything of interest and importance" (p. 493). Today, the majority of psychologists, both academics and practitioners, accept the argument that a purely natural-science approach is inadequate for understanding human behavior. Sperry (1993) referred to the cognitive revolution as "the recorded fact of a turning point in the history of science" (p. 880). In his Lifetime Contribution Award address to the American Psychological Association, he made an even stronger point: "I remain quite serious in suggesting that psychology is today turning the tables on physics and hard science and, with its cognitive revolution, is now leading the way in science to a more valid and more accurate paradigm for scientific and all causal explanation ... the cognitive revolution is a revolution for science" (Sperry, 1995, pp. 505–506).

Have cognitive models triumphed over their behavioral predecessors? Are there only two alternatives available for psychology, one way forward and one way back? Or are there other approaches to our subject that might prove more fruitful than either?

It is noticeable that cognition-oriented psychology is increasingly taken up where behaviorism is cast off. It has been argued that cognitive and behavioral models are so different as to be completely incommensurable. After all, the aim of behaviorism is to examine the relation between behavior and context, and the aim of cognitivism is to "establish the design of the internal machinery through whose functioning organisms are capable of behaving in context" (Schnaitter, 1987a, p. 1). At least in a historical sense, it appears that the two cannot coexist peacefully; one of them is taking over from the other.

A survey of members of the Association for Advancement of Behavior Therapy found that 71% described their theoretical orientation as cognitive or cognitive–behavioral (Craighead, 1990), although a small but vocal group of noncognitive behaviorists remains within that organization (Sweet, 1994). In 1990, the Association's journal *Behavior Therapy*, one of the most highly regarded journals in the social sciences (Awad, 1990), removed the words "behavior therapy and behavior modification" from its byline and replaced them with "behavioral and cognitive sciences." Two recent archival studies (Dobson, Beamish, & Taylor, 1992; Hawkins, Kashden, Hansen, & Sadd, 1992) have shown a steady increase in references to cognitive variables over 20 years of *Behavior Therapy* and presentations at the annual convention of the Association for Advancement of Behavior Therapy. On the wider scene, Baer, Wolf, and Risley (1987) estimated that behaviorists comprised approximately 2% of American psychologists. In applied and clinical psychology, cognitive models are increasingly becoming the norm and noncognitive theorists a minority with whom the mainstream has little in common. Are psychologists right to reject behaviorism, and if they are, is cognitivism the only alternative?

THE PRIMACY OF COGNITION

The concept that conscious thought is primary to human action has a long and respectable intellectual tradition. In its modern development, it can be traced to Descartes' philosophical treatment of free will, of the dual nature of mind and body, and in particular to his contention that "the essence of a person is thinking" (Rée, 1974, p. 118).

Humans, according to Descartes, were different from all other creatures in that they possessed a soul, which was nonmaterial (although it had a physical location, in the pineal gland). The soul was responsible for thought, volition, and emotion. Other animals did not have souls and therefore did not have free will. Rather, they responded in a mechanical way to environmental and biological stimuli. Human beings worked on entirely different principles, with all their actions guided by the internal but incorporeal will.

The modern computer metaphor, which treats the mind as an abstract set of instructions controlling the corporeal body, is a contemporary rephrasing of Descartes' ideas (Costall, 1991; Hineline, 1992). Despite the arguments (e.g., Sperry, 1993) that the emergent-process models of the new cognitive theories are not dualistic, it is hard to see contemporary cognitive models of behavior as anything other than reinforcing the philosophical divide between the physical and the mental (Hergenhahn, 1994).

The concept of the centrality of thought to human action has a tradition that can be traced to sources well before Descartes, for example in the much earlier teachings of the Stoic philosophers. Epictetus (ca. 50 – 125 AD) is perhaps the most familiar of these. His contention that "what disturbs human beings is not the things themselves, but their opinions about things" (Xenakis, 1969, p. 21) would have an oddly familiar ring to many modern cognitive–behavioral therapists. Our entire intellectual heritage could be said to rest on the assumption that thinking about thinking is the way to understand human beings and that understanding human beings is the first step to understanding the world (Schnaitter, 1987b).

Returning to contemporary social, applied, and cognitive psychology, a bewildering array of mutually contradictory models of human choices and human behavior exists, and a large literature is dedicated to the comparison, revision, integration, and disintegration of these models across an enormous range of behavioral domains. These theories differ in their scope and emphasis and in the hypothesized central variables. However, they are based on a common set of assumptions (Holt & Lee, 1989; Weinstein, 1993) and derived from a single philosophical tradition. All are based on the assumption that conscious thought is a direct cause of human behavior. It is the most important cause of human behavior, and the only one that psychologists ought to study. Economic, social, and environmental influences on choice and freedom are largely ignored by contemporary social and cognitive theories (Norman & Conner, 1993).

Chapter 2 provides a detailed examination of one of these modern models, self-efficacy theory. This was selected as an illustration because it is arguably the most popular and successful of this general class of model, as well as one that spans both the social and the clinical arenas, originally developed as a model of therapeutic change (Bandura, 1977) and later expanded as a more general theory (Bandura, 1986, 1991). Self-efficacy theory is taken as a specific illustration of the underlying arguments and the fundamental problems common to a number of similar models.

Cognition in Contemporary Social and Clinical Psychology

The most basic common assumption is that cognitions, of which the actor is conscious or can become conscious through introspection, are the immediate causes of human behavior. The theories, therefore, hold that assessment of the relevant cognitions, if done cleverly enough, will allow completely accurate prediction of behavior. Those that guide a large amount of research and have a respected tradition include the health belief model (Janz & Becker, 1984); protection motivation theory (e.g., Maddux & Rogers, 1983); the theory of reasoned action (e.g., Fishbein & Ajzen, 1975); and the theory of planned behavior (e.g., Ajzen & Madden, 1986); Triandis' model of behavioral choice (Triandis, 1980); and the many different aspects of attribution theory (e.g., Jaspars, Fincham, & Hewstone, 1983).

Attribution theory (e.g., Heider, 1944) and dissonance theory (e.g., Brehm & Cohen, 1962; Festinger, 1957) are supported by decades of research predicated on the assumption that social behavior is determined by attitudes and beliefs, themselves the result of cognitive interpretation of experience. According to these models, the real world is relevant only peripherally, as the raw material from which the individual constructs a subjective world (Bruner, 1986). Therefore, it is held, efforts to understand social behavior should focus primarily on cognitive interpretations of events and not on the events themselves. As Wyatt (1990) put it, the field "equates 'scientific' psychology to 'cognitive' psychology" (p. 1181) and thus defines everything else out of existence as a legitimate topic for research.

Cognitively oriented models in the field of clinical psychology include those of Beck (e.g., 1984), Ellis (1962), and Meichenbaum (1974). Cognitive behavior therapy, as a therapeutic approach, uses an eclectic range of therapeutic procedures, but its primary aim, whatever the specific of a particular school of therapy, is to identify and correct inappropriate cognitions. Because it is assumed that cognitions are the primary cause of behavior and of emotion, any subsequent improvement in emotional state is attributed to the effect of changes in cognition. For example, Ellis (e.g., 1977, 1987, 1993) maintained that irrational beliefs lead to inappropriate interpretations of situations, persons, and their behavior and that these interpretations (and not objective events in the material world, such as terminal illness or the loss of a loved one) are the cause of most emotional distress. In particular, absolutist thinking is crucial in the development of depression and must be changed if depression is to be alleviated (Ellis, 1987).

Thus, the cognitive therapeutic frameworks assume that human behavior is driven by conscious thought, or at least by cognitions that are readily amenable to verbal description when the behaver is asked about them. With Epictetus, they assume further that problems are largely caused by illogical, irrational, dysfunctional, or otherwise faulty cognitions. It follows from these assumptions that emotional disorders and behavioral problems are best treated by intervention strategies that aim to alter cognitions (Holt & Lee, 1989). Although circumstances may be unfortunate, the individual's reaction to those circumstances is the real problem, and it is the proper role of the psychologist to help the individual to change that reaction.

The theoretical and therapeutic model of Beck (e.g., 1991) is superficially similar, although closer examination reveals important differences. Beck did not claim that cognitions cause depression but that they are an integral part of the depressive state. "To conclude that cognitions cause depression is analogous to asserting that delusions cause schizophrenia" (Beck, 1991, p. 371). However, Beck's view on the causes of depression is by no means a definitive one. "I have considered the activation of the [negative] schemas to be a mechanism by which the depression develops, not as the cause. The cause may be in any combination of biological, genetic, stress, or personality factors " (Beck, 1991, p. 371). Although this statement raises a number of possible areas for investigation, it is clearly not intended to be the last word on the development of depression, and Beck's therapeutic strategies still focus on the identification and modification of cognitions.

THEORETICAL PROBLEMS

Modern theories of social behavior are based on the untested assumption that human activity is largely determined by cognitive variables. Physiology, environment, and behavior are peripheral to the understanding of cognition, which is central to the understanding of human nature. This consensus may be adduced as evidence that psychology is succeeding in becoming an integrated field of inquiry. However, these assumptions, and by extension, the theories themselves, are open to question, and sound reasons exist for maintaining a debate on the role of cognition in behavior.

The theories that take the currently dominant approach to the subject matter of psychology suffer from four major problems. First, the theories are inadequate at a formal level: They are incomplete because of a failure to define their components and to identify their boundaries. Second, application of the theories is perforce unsatisfactory. Because of vagueness at a formal level, there are no unambiguous ways of transferring the general hypothetical constructs into specific questionnaire items or intervention strategies for specific experimental or clinical settings. Thus, the link between theory and application is always inexact, making empirical tests of the theories themselves impossible. Third, the strategies of therapy and of social influence derived from the models are highly variable in empirical success. The models fail to predict the circumstances in which they will be successful or to provide clear directions for improvement. Fourth, these models are based on untested assumptions about the centrality of cognition to human behavior.

Currently popular theories are not scientific accounts of human behavior and cannot be translated into scientifically based therapeutic techniques (Lee, 1989b). They rely for their apparent explanatory power on ill-defined, unobservable cognitive variables. They then assume that these cognitive variables interact, in equally ill-defined ways, to produce a cognitive outcome. This cognitive outcome is then argued to be the proximal determinant of actual behavior, but, as it and all its components are undefined and unobservable, the argument is untestable and has no practical application.

For example, the health belief model (Janz & Becker, 1984) hypothesizes that four major sets of beliefs — beliefs about the seriousness of a condition, beliefs about one's susceptibility to that condition, beliefs about the efficacy of preventative actions, and beliefs about the barriers to those actions — determine whether a person will engage in a particular health-related action or not. The four beliefs arise from unspecified previous experiences and may be modified at any time by other unspecified experiences.

The ability of a model such as this to explain, predict, or provide strategies to modify human behavior is illusory (Lee, 1989b). It is based on the sensible-sounding notion that our choice of behavior in any situation arises from a complex interaction among different types of attitudes, but it lacks any precision. Such models seem plausible, but their explanatory power is spurious (Staddon, 1984). They provide no unambiguous definitions of crucial variables, nor are there satisfactory methods for measurement (Kazdin, 1978), nor is the nature of the interactions among the variables specified. Thus, they provide likely sounding but essentially vague descriptions of our subjective experience. It is impossible that models that are so ambiguous could provide a scientific account of human behavior (Eysenck, 1978; Lee, 1987, 1989b; Skinner, 1977, 1987). In particular, one cannot make any firm prediction about the behavioral effects of any specific combination of scores on scales designed to measure the hypothesized cognitive variables (Lee, 1989b), let alone predict behavior from knowledge of the individual's personal history.

Influences on Cognition

The first question that arises in a critical examination of models of this type is that of the process by which component cognitions arise. Where do particular beliefs, attitudes and opinions come from? How do events in the real world affect them? The issue of which sources of information will influence cognitive variables, and the nature of that influence, is generally not addressed coherently, if it is addressed at all.

For example, self-efficacy theory (e.g., Bandura, 1977) and its development in social cognitive theory (Bandura, 1986) hypothesize that the cognitions relevant to choosing a particular course of action are influenced by personal experiences, vicarious experiences, verbal and other symbolic information, and perceptions of physiological states. However, this is as far as the theory goes. There are no predictions of the direction or extent of influence. Thus, it is impossible to predict the effect that any specific combination of experiences might have on self-efficacy or to hypothesize, at any level of precision beyond that suggested by common sense, that any particular event will affect the cognitive variables in any particular way. This and related models propose that experiences and events have effects on cognitions, but they fail to provide any way of predicting what the effect will be for any particular set of circumstances.

Interactions Among Cognitions

As well as naming some hypothetical variables and arguing that they are related to behavioral choices, many of these models argue that these variables combine to produce a single cognitive outcome, which in turn determines behavior. The details of this cognitive outcome vary among theories. Bandura (1986) argued that the crucial cognitive outcome is self-efficacy. The theory of reasoned action (Fishbein & Ajzen, 1976), theory of planned behavior (Ajzen, 1991) and the more complex model of Triandis (1980) hold that cognitive variables combine to produce a behavioral intention. Protection motivation theory (Rogers, 1983), related specifically to health actions, argues for protection motivation as the final common pathway. The argument is basically the same in each case. A variety of component variables arise from a variety of classes of experiences and combine in some way to produce a single cognition that has a direct effect on behavior (Weinstein, 1993).

Development and testing of predictions concerning these composite cognitive variables is, however, impossible. Relations between the cognitive components and the composite outcome are not specified. Thus, the theories are too imprecise for any but the vaguest predictions about the outcome on the basis of information about the hypothesized cognitive components. The effects that a change in any component variable might have on the outcome variable cannot be predicted. This severely limits both the practical applicability of such theories and the possibility of testing them. For example, the health belief model cannot predict the sexual behavior of a person who believes AIDS to be extremely serious, feels somewhat susceptible, and sees substantial barriers to preventive action. Will this person use a condom or not? Your guess is as good as mine. In developing a workable theory of human behavior, it is not enough simply to invent a number of hypothetical variables, give them names, and propose that they will combine; the nature of the combination must be specified.

So far, then, these models may be characterized as frameworks that hypothesize that events in the material world have effects on crucial cognitions but fail to specify precisely what these effects will be; they then hypothesize that these cognitions are integrated to produce a composite cognition but again fail to specify the nature of the process. Thus, we have vagueness upon vagueness, attractive metaphors perhaps, but nothing that can be regarded as a useful description of how people choose their actions.

Observable Effects of Cognitions

A third stage in these theories is also problematic, and that concerns the relation between the composite cognitive variable and behavior. Self-efficacy theory (e.g., Bandura, 1986), for example, holds that efficacy expectations are the proximal determinants of behavior. If we had a perfect measure of self-efficacy, it would also be an accurate predictor of behavior. The empirical evidence shows quite variable relations between measured efficacy and measured behavior, but this can be explained away in terms of difficulties with measurement and assessment.

Of course, this characterization is a vast oversimplification of a complex argument that takes other issues into account. For example, Bandura (1982) argued that behavioral capacity and environmental incentive must be present for the hypothesized close relation between self-efficacy and behavior to obtain. Other models are more circumspect about the relation between the composite variable and behavior but no more satisfactory. Fishbein and Ajzen (1976), for example, argued that behavioral intention is an immediate precursor of behavior but that many other variables may influence the relation between intention and behavior.

They argued that the relation between measured cognition and observed behavior is affected by measurement issues, including the level of specificity of the questions and the time between measurement of behavioral intention and observation of behavior. They also pointed to the role of more substantive influences, such as the degree to which the behavior is under volitional control and to which the intention remains stable. The role of previous behavior in related situations, conceptualized as habit strength, was also included in Triandis' (1980) elaboration of the model. These propositions, like the theories themselves, sound reasonable and may give the illusion that the problem of predicting behavior from cognition has been adequately dealt with. However, all they really do is introduce more unmeasurable constructs.

The assessment of relevant behavioral or environmental factors is not perceived by cognitive theorists as integral to a complete model of human functioning. Rather, the view of these theorists seems to be that these variables interfere with the relation between cognitive variables and behavior; they are inconvenient contaminants that must be controlled through careful assessment and clever experimental designs, not variables that a psychologist should study as legitimate influences on human behavior. It might even be said that their role is to function as escape clauses for times when behavior fails to match the theory. The practical effect of this approach is to provide a vague but reasonable-sounding explanation for situations in which cognitive variables do not predict behavior; the theoretical effect is to affirm the place of cognition as the only variable of interest to psychologists, reducing all other variables to the status of external and theoretically irrelevant inconveniences. Thus, cognition is defined not simply as the variable of central importance in understanding human behavior, but as the only legitimate topic of study.

A Fundamental Problem

These criticisms have been made and responded to before, but the attempts of many influential researchers to deal with problems of empirical failure and conceptual vagueness are often theoretically unsatisfying. For example, a number of theorists (e.g., Lewinsohn, Hoberman, Teri, & Hautzinger, 1985; Olinger, Kuiper, & Shaw, 1987) proposed expanded cognitive models with complex interactive structures and chains of reciprocal causality. This, however, is only a further compounding of the underlying problem. Models that increase complexity without increasing precision and that invoke additional hypothetical variables but are still vague as to how these arise, how they should be measured, how they interact with each other, and how they relate to behavior are of no help in the prediction or understanding of that behavior (Coyne & Gotlib, 1986; Lee, 1989b).

Proposing the existence of more hypothetical variables misses the basic problem that the variables are not adequately defined, their relations are not defined, and we have no satisfactory ways of assessing them. The fundamental empirical problem with these models is that there is no way of predicting what specific actions might arise from particular levels of the hypothesized variables, and this empirical problem arises directly from a lack of theoretical precision (Lee, 1989b).

Corrigan (1990) put the argument that this problem is soluble. It is a problem of research design rather than a fundamental weakness in the models themselves. The use of complex multivariate statistical techniques should allow us to make guesses about the relations among these variables. Armed with these preliminary hypotheses, we could then test specific models. In this way the models would be strengthened, and we would eventually develop better and more precise theories.

Research attempting to refine the nature of the relations among cognitive variables has been going on for some time. Much of this research has been rigorously conducted and has used large samples and complex statistical techniques (e.g., Feltz & Mugno, 1983; Godding & Glasgow, 1985). I have even conducted some of it myself (e.g., Lee, 1984a,1984b). However, a relatively large proportion of the variance in behavior is still left unexplained by cognitive variables (e.g., Baer, Holt, & Lichtenstein, 1986), and observable variables such as previous behaviors are frequently found to be more accurate predictors (e.g., Feltz & Mugno, 1983; Lee, 1983). This suggests that an exclusive emphasis on cognition may be misplaced.

Theories with a basis in behavior theory can provide alternatives to the more baroque cognitive models (e.g., Biglan, 1987; Rachlin, Logue, Gibbon, & Frankel, 1986; Tryon, 1982), although they do not have the same popularity. As I discuss in chapter 8, this reluctance to accept noncognitive views of the human being may have deep cultural roots. Schnaitter (1987a) pointed to the epistemological tradition that has focused the attention of philosophers throughout millennia primarily on thought, rather than on the external world, and argued that this historical context makes a thought-centred approach to human action seem natural and inevitable. More specifically, Baer et al. (1987) argued that psychologists generally find noncognitive explanations of human behavior unreinforcing and that this is why they are not widely accepted. Even so, finding something unpalatable is not sufficient grounds for declaring it wrong.

METHODOLOGICAL PROBLEMS

My argument so far has concentrated on theoretical deficiencies. In this section, I extend this argument to examine its relation to the widely acknowledged problems with the measurement of these hypothetical variables. A lack of conceptual precision leads to insurmountable difficulties at the practical level. Theoretical niceties matter practically.

Procedurally, the most immediate implication of the theoretical problems of vagueness and ambiguity is that it is extremely difficult to develop research questionnaires that accurately reflect the concepts. When specific questions, comprehensible to research subjects, are devised, the differences between conceptually distinct variables can become very hard to see. Mullen, Hersey, and Iverson (1987), for example, comparing three social psychological models, commented that "numerous respondents objected to the apparent similarity of belief strength and belief importance questions. They said 'but I already answered that,' when asked about the importance of each belief they had rated earlier. This perception that the questions were the same seemed to carry over into the answers"(p. 978).

This experience is one I have shared, for example in research assessing efficacy and outcome expectations (Lee, 1984a, 1984b). These studies showed very high correlations between efficacy and outcome expectations, despite theoretical arguments (e.g., Bandura, 1982) that they should be largely independent of each other. Concepts that appear quite distinct may lose that distinctness when converted into questions in everyday English, with all its imprecisions and shades of meaning. Schwarz (1990), discussing verbal reports in general, argued that respondents are unlikely to engage in sophisticated semantic analysis but will "respond to the gist of the question rather than to its exact wording" (p. 101). Thus, a respondent without prior knowledge of the theory under investigation may be quite unaware of the subtle shades of meaning that the researcher has hoped to convey.

For example, a subject asked to make ratings of efficacy and outcome expectations about his or her ability to handle a snake might be asked the following pair of questions:

1. "Rate your degree of confidence in your ability to pick up the snake."
2. "Rate how positive or negative you would expect the outcome to be if you picked up the snake."

The subject might reason as follows: "How confident am I that I can pick up this snake? I am a bit uneasy about snakes, so let's say 40%. Now, question two. How positive or negative would I feel? Well, I have already said I am a bit uneasy. Uneasiness is negative. It's the same question really, so I will say 40% again" (assuming first, that subjects go through any sort of reasoning process when faced with a questionnaire and second, that this reasoning process has any relation at all to their responses).

To take another example, the health belief model hypothesizes four relevant cognitive variables: perceived severity, perceived susceptibility, effectiveness of action, and barriers to taking action. To the researcher, these are obviously distinct; however, it is feasible that a subject, lacking specific knowledge of the hypothetical variables and the underlying theory, could consider a question seriously but still answer in a way that mixes the concepts (Ronis, 1992).

Thus, a subject in a survey of beliefs about skin cancer might be faced with a severity question: "How serious a condition is basal cell carcinoma?" He or she may draw on personal experience of the condition. Basal cell carcinomas, the subject will probably know, are very easily treated if detected early. Friends who have had the condition have undergone a short, painless treatment and have been completely cured. Clearly something that is so readily cured is not a serious condition. This seems a quite sensible way of approaching the question, yet it confuses the apparently distinct categories of severity and the effectiveness of action.

An effectiveness of action question might read, "How effective is maximum-protection sunblock in the prevention of skin cancer?" The subject may know that consistent use of sunblock will prevent the development of cancer but may reason that she and her friends hardly ever use sunblock because they like to be tanned. Such a person may rate sunblock as not an effective way to prevent cancer. After all, in her experience, people don't use it, and sunblock cannot prevent cancer if people don't use it. In this case, we have a quite reasonable response that combines effectiveness of action with perceptions of barriers to that action.

DESCRIPTION VERSUS EXPLANATION

A further problem with models that focus on cognitions and rely on self-report is that they deal entirely with hypothetical constructs, and their relation to reality is impossible to assess. Therefore, there is little to prevent a proliferation of theories postulating subtly different cognitions with different relations between them (Weinstein, 1993). Cummings, Becker, and Maile (1980) identified 14 different models that related cognitive variables to health-related behaviors, involving 109 variable names, and concluded that "many investigators have long felt that the actual number of truly distinct concepts ... is considerably lower " (p. 123). Cummings et al. (1980) also stressed that the process of describing and naming hypothetical variables need not be related to understanding the causes of behavior.

A more recent review of social–psychological approaches to exercise promotion (Maddux, 1993) came to a very similar conclusion. The competing models have a great deal of overlap, and they all deal with the same basic set of variables, divided in slightly different ways.

Recent years have shown a rise in pragmatic clinical research at the expense of theoretically relevant work (Omer & Dar, 1992). This emphasis has led to a situation in which "there may be merely a collection of very different types of therapies that are called 'cognitive–behavioral' therapies, but that have no interesting common properties" (Erwin, 1992, p. 152). The same criticism may be made of social psychological models, because they have no coherent theoretical basis.

Eifert and Plaud (1993) made a similar point, suggesting that the adoption of intervening-variable models in therapeutic settings is not justified by theoretical development. They asked, "where ... have the conceptual foundations of the various cognitive–behavioral theories and treatments been adequately defined and elaborated on?" (p. 103) and warned that "increased preoccupation with hypothesised inner processes will weaken the behavior therapy movement unless theories about private events are appropriately related to and integrated with basic behavioral concepts and research findings" (p. 103).

The distinction between post hoc, metaphorical descriptions and actual explanations of behavior is one that is important to maintain (Lee, 1989b). Kimble (1989) criticized the tendency of "intervening-variable" psychologists to confuse concept formation with explanation and made the point that disputes about such intervening variables are arguments about definitions, not about facts. Intervening variables are imaginary constructs, invented rather than discovered by the cognitive model builders.

Thus, a great deal of research with a cognitive orientation may be no more than the correlation of self-reports of hypothetical constructs with self-reports of other hypothetical constructs. In the words of Skinner (1977, p. 1), "cognitive psychologists (...) invent internal surrogates which become the subject matter of their science." The real world is forgotten in the development of increasingly abstruse models whose relation to objective reality is no longer a concern because objective reality has come to be considered irrelevant to the subject matter of psychology.

Skinner (1977) personified the antithesis of such an approach, arguing throughout his life that all mediational models are by their nature unscientific and that the invocation of thoughts, intentions, or feelings to explain behavior has an inherent circularity (see Skinner, 1990, for his final public words on the subject). All mental processes, he argued, are metaphors for observable, or potentially observable, processes that are not yet fully understood, and their labeling and apparent reification is inappropriate, misleading, and retrogressive. Skinner's logic and his intellectual courage are convincing. However, many have responded that, until these potentially observable processes are actually understood, the metaphorical concepts are a convenient way of referring to processes that appear important in understanding human actions, a simple short-hand for highly complex biochemical and neurological processes.

A major problem with this argument, though, is the apparent ease with which we can forget that the structures and processes described by such cognitive models do not exist. Inventing unobservable processes may seem advantageous in the short term, but in the long term this approach hinders a more scientific and theoretical understanding (Skinner, 1990). There is a danger that the widespread acceptance of frameworks that use imaginary concepts may lead to a situation in which models that describe processes come to be mistaken for theories that explain them (Skinner, 1989). Although metaphors are useful, it is important to remember that they are not explanations but merely convenient labels for processes yet to be explained.

CONCLUSION

The basic argument of this chapter is that cognitive theories of psychology suffer from an insurmountable flaw: They rely on undefined and unobservable variables to explain behavior. The undefined nature of the variables, the lack of consensus concerning subtle differences between differently named variables, and the unspecified and unobservable nature of their interactions produce fundamental problems. These problems mean that the models are useless in understanding or predicting behavior, although they may be seductive ways of talking about that behavior afterwards.

In summary, the currently popular social–cognitive theories have the following flaws: They postulate the existence of cognitive variables but are unclear as to how they arise from external experiences and events; they postulate that cognitive variables interact to produce composite cognitions but are unclear as to how; and they suggest that this resulting composite cognition would, under perfect circumstances, predict behavior but again are unclear as to the effects of other variables on this relation. Thus, it is impossible to make precise predictions as to what cognitions will arise in a particular person from a particular set of events, how these cognitions will interact with each other, and what behavior will occur as a result. Although such models have the appearance of taking the complexity of human decision making into account, they are of no actual use in explaining or predicting behavior. In the following chapter, I illustrate this argument by examining one of the most popular and successful of these models in more detail.

Chapter 2

Science and Explanation:
Distinguishing Between Commonsense
Description and Scientific Explanation

Common sense is a valuable but potentially dangerous resource for the psychologist.

—Fletcher (1984, p. 203)

The opening chapter introduced a general argument that many contemporary cognitively based models are unsatisfactory as scientific explanations of human action. In this chapter I aim to make the argument more specific, using the influential self-efficacy and social–cognitive models of Bandura (1977, 1986) to illustrate the problems with theories of this type. This chapter examines the formal theoretical difficulties with such models and discusses empirical evidence suggesting that such theories fail to provide an understanding of behavior that exceeds that of more parsimonious theories.

It is important to emphasize that I have chosen self-efficacy theory because of its notable success and widespread acceptance and not because it is in any way a bad example. The points I wish to make apply to many models, and illustrations are drawn from others where appropriate. Self-efficacy theory, because of its familiarity to most readers, is used to illustrate the general argument, that the lack of a scientific basis leads inevitably to a lack of internal clarity and to a lack of genuine practical application.

SELF-EFFICACY THEORY

Self-efficacy theory, originally proposed by Bandura (1977), has gained widespread acceptance in clinical and applied psychology. In common with many other cognitive, social learning, and systems-based frameworks, it has apparent practical appeal. A scan of publications in mainstream psychological journals finds empirical work using measures of self-efficacy in almost every application of psychology.

The initial work concentrated almost exclusively on demonstration projects with clients with severe snake phobia (e.g., Bandura, Adams, & Beyer, 1977; Bandura, Reese, & Adams, 1982). Since then, there has been expansion and development with other clinical populations (e.g., Katz, Stout, Taylor, Horne, & Agras, 1983; Segal & Marshall, 1986). More recent research has extended the model to health-related behaviors in the nonclinical population, including such diverse activities as weight loss (Bernier & Avard, 1986); smoking cessation (e.g., Haaga & Stewart, 1993; Kavanagh, Pierce, Lo, & Shelley, 1993; Mudde, Kok, & Strecher, 1995); exercise adoption (e.g., Marcus & Owen, 1992; Wurtele & Maddux, 1987); condom use (Jemmott, Jemmott, Spears, Hewitt, & Cruz-Collins, 1992; Wulfert & Wan, 1993); preparation for medical procedures (Gattuso, Litt, & Fitzgerald, 1992); and coping with chronic medical conditions (e.g., Padgett, 1991; Schiaffino, Revenson, & Gibofsky, 1991).

Recent publications have expanded the applications even further, dealing with such disparate topics as maintenance of counseling relationships (Longo, Lent, & Brown, 1992); sporting performance (e.g., George, 1994; Taylor, 1989); career decision-making (e.g., Church, Teresa, Rosebrook, & Szendre, 1992; Lauver & Jones, 1991; Luzzo, 1993); vocational interest (Lapan, Boggs & Morrill, 1989); performance at work (Sadri & Robertson, 1993) and in study (Hackett, Betz, Casas, & Rocha-Singh, 1992); adaptation to computerized technology (Gist, Schwoerer & Rosen, 1989); success in military training (Tannenbaum, Mathieu, Salas, & Cannon-Bowers, 1991); avoidance of professional burnout (Meier, 1983); adjustment to retirement (Holahan, Holahan, & Belk, 1984); and even the avoidance of seasickness (Eden & Zuk, 1995).

Overall, it would be a fair summary of this literature to say that many investigations have found efficacy expectations to be reasonably accurate predictors of behavior. The model has also had a wider influence. Other social-learning theorists have included the concept of self-efficacy in the development or refinement of complex models of the process of behavior change (e.g., DiClemente, Prochaska, & Gibertini, 1985; Maddux & Rogers, 1983; Marlatt & Gordon, 1985), reinterpreted existing social psychological concepts in terms of self-efficacy theory (e.g., Sanna, 1992), or added self-efficacy to existing theories (Lerner & Locke, 1995; Silver, Mitchell, & Gist, 1995). Research produces results that generally support the model, and criticism of the theory is rare. Are we to conclude from this state of affairs that self-efficacy has answered its detractors and now has only to beware of imitations?

Self-Efficacy Theory: Theoretical Issues

Criticisms of self-efficacy and related theories still need to be made. Theories of this type, despite their apparent value and their widespread popularity, are fundamentally invalid. They rely for their apparent explanatory power on unpredictable interactions among hypothetical variables that cannot be observed and are not operationally defined (e.g., Eysenck, 1978; Lee, 1987; Skinner, 1977, 1987). All definitions are circular; no variable can be assessed independent of other variables identified by the theory, and many crucial variables are not observable either directly or through their effects.

Bandura's (1977) initial description of the self-efficacy concept elicited strong positive reactions (e.g., Kazdin, 1978; Kendall & Korgeski, 1979; Wilson, 1978), together with critical debate (e.g., Borkovec, 1978; Eysenck, 1978; Lang, 1978; Tryon, 1981). The model was adjudged, then as now, as potentially useful in a range of settings, to assess progress and assist in the selection of therapeutic goals (e.g., Clark, Abrams, Niaura, Eaton, & Rossi, 1991). However, some basic questions concerning the theory as an explanation of human behavior were raised then and have yet to be answered. Difficulties involved in the unambiguous measurement of self-efficacy (e.g., Kazdin, 1978; Wilson, 1978) were discussed, and the point was made that precise and unambiguous measurement of crucial variables is a necessary precondition for theory testing.

Critical debate has more recently concentrated on matters of emphasis within self-efficacy theory. The relative importance of different variables (e.g., Eastman & Marzillier, 1984), methodological variations (e.g., Cervone, 1985; Kirsch, 1986; Lee & Bobko, 1994), and terminology (e.g., Kirsch, 1986) have been examined. More general, but still firmly within the cognitive frameworks that underlie self-efficacy theory, have been discussions of the relation among self-efficacy variables and cognitive variables derived from other models such as the health belief model, the theory of reasoned action, and related theories (e.g., Dzewaltowski, 1989; Dzewaltowski, Noble, & Shaw, 1990; Kimiecik, 1992; Miller, Carlyle, & Pease, 1992; Seydel, Taal, & Wiegman, 1990; Tedesco, Keffer, Davis, & Christersson, 1993; Tedesco, Keffer, & Fleck-Kandath, 1991; Weinstein, 1993). These authors have questioned the details of one specific model but have implicitly accepted the underlying assumptions of all the models, that cognitive variables are central in causing behavior and that studying cognitive variables is the only logical way to understand human beings. Questions regarding the validity of the basic assumptions are less often asked and are increasingly seen as irrelevant or ill informed.

Bandura has always been open to comment and willing to reply to criticism (see, for example, Bandura, 1978, 1980, 1984, 1986, 1991, 1995), responding to specific points and expanding on the theory. Although his theoretical perspective has developed over time, he has consistently argued that the theory identifies a cognitive variable (i.e., self-efficacy) that is the proximal determinant of behavior. Although an essential feature of Bandura's model is a complex process of reciprocal influence among variables, self-efficacy is described not simply as a useful and accessible predictor but as the most immediate cause of behavior. The theory is explicitly described as more than just a descriptive model, as an explanatory theory of behavior, and it is at this level that insurmountable problems arise.

Levels of Explanation. It is important to distinguish between a model's presentation of a believable but essentially metaphorical description of a process and its ability to explain that process. Although self-efficacy theory appears to be a valuable tool clinically and empirically, much of its apparent explanatory value is illusory and is based on a confusion of description with explanation.

The tendency to take a reasonable-sounding description of how events may occur and then assume it to be an explanation of those events is understandable but is not logical. The naming of a variable, however sensible it sounds, does not cause it to exist. Cognitive variables are constructed by cognitive theorists, not discovered by them. Whereas self-efficacy and related theories may appeal to common sense, this is not necessarily an indication of their accuracy or scientific value (Kelley, 1992).

It is true that self-efficacy does predict behavior in relatively uncomplicated contexts with a fair degree of accuracy. However, at the level of explaining the processes involved in behaving and in behavior change, rather than simply providing one of a number of possible descriptions of them, it does not increase our understanding. To state that a person behaved in a particular way primarily because of self-efficacy is not a scientific explanation.

Reliance on Unobservable Variables. Self-efficacy theory, like other social cognitive theories, emphasizes expectations and beliefs as determinants of behavior. In particular, people have specific, accurately reportable expectations concerning their ability to perform any task, and these expectations determine action. Provided the individual has "appropriate skills and adequate incentives" (Bandura, 1977, p. 194) for a particular task, behavior is caused by efficacy expectations.

Although Bandura (e.g., 1981, 1983, 1984, 1986) argued consistently against simple models that propose unidirectional determinants of behavior, he made it clear that he regarded efficacy expectations as causally prior to behavior: "Self-percepts of efficacy are not simply inert predictors of future behavior. People's beliefs about their capabilities influence how they behave" (Bandura, 1984, p. 242). Although efficacy expectations are not the only factor that determines behavior, the theory quite clearly accords them a central causal role.

The model may appear to have advantages over less complex models of behavior. In particular, it suggests a potential common mechanism by which a variety of experiences or therapeutic strategies could influence behavior in similar ways. This common mechanism is a cognitive one, which, as has been pointed out (e.g., Hickey, 1994; Sampson, 1981), appeals to a view of the human being, popular among psychologists and dominant in Western culture, as primarily driven by individual and subjective interpretations of events rather than by events themselves.

The major flaw of proposals of this kind is that they are based on undefined and unobservable interactions between imprecisely defined variables. It is important to stress that this flaw is not unique to self-efficacy theory but is also a weakness of the other cognitive models under consideration. Influential theoreticians (e.g., Mahoney, 1974) have argued that it is both legitimate and necessary to infer the existence of unobservable processes to understand human behavior. However, making such inferences causes more difficulties than it solves; the unverifiable nature of the models that result renders them unscientific, and their vagueness and ambiguity render them unworkable (e.g., Lee, 1987; Skinner, 1977).

Lack of Precision. The brief description of the process by which efficacy expectations develop highlights a major weakness of the theory: The process by which the synthesis of information takes place is not specified. No model predicts the weighting of various types of information. Thus, there is no way of predicting efficacy and no way of developing techniques that reliably alter efficacy expectations. Because of the large number of potential influences and the lack of a rigorous model, almost any level of self-efficacy could arise from almost any set of circumstances. Thus, it is not simply that self-efficacy has no material existence, but also that it cannot be reliably inferred from any observable event or process, that renders the theory unscientific.

Furthermore, the problem of undefined and unobservable interactions is not confined to the development of the efficacy expectation. A similar problem arises in describing how efficacy expectations interact with other variables. For example, Bandura argued that skill levels and incentives are also important influences on behavior. Again, the model reflects the complexity and variability we perceive in human behavior and accords with the satisfying view that people are very complicated. However, it is of no actual use. Again, naming of variables has substituted for explanation.

There is no framework for specifying how skills and incentives might be assessed independently of the behavior they are supposed to affect nor for identifying the way in which efficacy expectations interact with these other variables. Thus, there is no way of predicting what behavior will result from any particular combination of skill, efficacy, and incentive. The vagueness of the basic constructs precludes the successful development of such a framework. What, for example, is "incentive"? How is it distinct from outcome expectations, from the perceived benefits of action, from health protection motivation? Again, applications must be less than reliable because of theoretical weakness.

The theory and other related theories postulate a large number of unobservable processes and argue that they interact in an unspecified manner to produce observable behavior. The invocation of unobservable processes is not sufficient to render a theory unworkable, but a theory must specify a reliable means of inferring those unobservables from other, observable variables, and this is what self-efficacy and related theories have failed to do. The lack of precision means that hypotheses cannot be developed to test these theories. It is almost impossible to come up with an outcome that could not be explained, post hoc, by self-efficacy theory. To be scientific, a theory must specify not only what will happen but also what will not happen.

This also means that techniques that reliably assist in dealing with human problems cannot be developed systematically. If a therapeutic technique is shown to affect behavior, self-efficacy theory does not allow us to understand why or how it has done so, beyond the unhelpful assertion that it must have enhanced self-efficacy. Thus, the potential for that technique's development and refinement is limited by the theoretical inadequacy of the model.

Measuring Efficacy Expectations. Even the end product of the hypothesized process, the efficacy expectation itself, has proved difficult to measure and to distinguish from other types of self-report. The difficulties involved in unambiguous measurement of self-efficacy (e.g., Kazdin, 1978; Wilson, 1978) were discussed when the theory was first proposed, and the point was made that, without precise measurement, theory testing cannot produce clear-cut results. These issues have not been resolved.

Much of the theoretical research on self-efficacy in recent years has examined the relative importance of efficacy expectations and other cognitive variables in the prediction of behavior (e.g., Hackett, 1985; Kavanagh & Bower, 1985; Maddux, Norton, & Stoltenberg, 1986; Seydel et al., 1990; Tedesco et al., 1991) and on how efficacy expectations differ from other cognitions (e.g., Godding & Glasgow, 1985; Kirsch, 1982; Leary & Atherton, 1986). Although the theoretical arguments have been well articulated and the empirical research is of unquestionably high quality, there is no sense in the research literature of the development of a coherent understanding of how these variables may relate to each other. This lack of a firm conclusion does not stem from any deficiency in the quality of the research; rather, it stems from a lack of clarity and objectivity in the theory itself.

The relation between efficacy and outcome expectations, for example, has been a subject of contention. Although several theories explain behavior in terms of expectancies, self-efficacy theory differs from some others (e.g., Abramson, Seligman, & Teasdale, 1978) in its focus on perceived ability to perform actions rather than on the expected outcome of particular actions. Bandura (e.g., 1978, 1982) argued that efficacy expectations and outcome expectations are conceptually distinct and can be distinguished empirically. Others (e.g., Eastman & Marzillier, 1984), however, have argued that the distinction between the two, in practical terms, is unclear. If the theory makes an important distinction between them, an inability to do so in practical terms renders it unworkable. This complaint again emphasizes the practical problems that arise directly from lack of theoretical precision.

The distinction between expectations about one's ability to do something and expectations about what will happen if one does it appears obvious, but when one actually comes to measure efficacy and outcome expectations, problems of definition arise. Maddux and Stanley (1986) argued that efficacy expectation refers to one's ability to perform a particular behavior and outcome expectation refers to the specific outcome expected. This may be appropriate in behavioral domains such as social interaction (e.g., Lee, 1984b), but in many situations there is no question about what the observable outcome of a particular behavior will be.

For example, many investigations of self-efficacy have dealt with snake phobia (e.g., Bandura et al., 1977; Lee, 1984a) and have involved participants in behavioral avoidance tests with a snake. In making judgments concerning most items in this test (e.g., "stand next to cage, looking at snake in cage"), there is no question as to the result of the action. The salient issue is not what will happen but how the target person expects that he or she might feel about performing the task. Lee (1984b), using a snake-handling task, therefore defined *outcome expectation* as the expected valence of the action and asked subjects to rate how positive or negative they would feel if they performed the task.

Sexton, Tuckman, and Crehan (1992) suggested that perhaps outcome expectation and outcome value need to be measured separately. Meier (1983) made a similar point, arguing for the existence of three types of expectation: efficacy expectations, outcome expectations, and reinforcement expectations. In this framework, a distinction is made between the objective result of an action (i.e., outcome expectation) and the extent to which the person finds the action and its result to be personally rewarding (i.e., reinforcement expectation). However, such a distinction is not always as clear-cut as it might seem.

It is unlikely that this debate will reach any conclusion if it continues at a semantic level or if different researchers continue to define and measure variables in different ways. Its basis, both practically and theoretically, can be questioned. Definitions of what constitutes a behavior, an outcome, and the valence or reinforcing value of that outcome are not at all clear cut. Take the example of the high jumper, used originally by Bandura (1978) and repeated elsewhere since then (e.g., Bandura, 1986; Eastman & Marzillier, 1984). One could argue, with Bandura, that " the belief that one can jump six feet is an efficacy judgment; the anticipated social recognition, applause, trophies, and self-satisfaction for such a performance constitute the outcome expectations" (Bandura, 1986, p. 391). If Bandura had included an outcome valence or reinforcement expectation in this description, he might have defined it as the belief that the social, material, and personal consequences are positively valued by the particular individual. Alternatively, and with equal logic, one could argue that efficacy expectations refer to confidence that one can perform the jump with correct form. Outcome expectations refer to the belief that somebody doing this would clear the bar, and reinforcement expectations, or outcome value, refers to the belief that clearing the bar would result in positive consequences.

It is difficult to see how one could distinguish the relative correctness of these two sets of definitions. The difference lies in how we choose to define any particular act. If an event can be a behavior, an outcome, or a consequence, depending on the way one chooses to describe it, then a model that makes a point of distinguishing between expectations concerning behaviors, outcomes, and the perceived value of those outcomes must break down.

Criticisms such as this have been raised before (e.g., Devins, 1992; Lee, 1992), but their behavioral effects are negligible. For example, Haaga and Stewart (1992b), in a discussion of the role of self-efficacy in smoking cessation, accepted that efficacy expectations and outcome expectations have been defined so ambiguously that the same belief could be considered an efficacy expectation or an outcome expectation, depending on the researcher's perspective. However, they argued that "this indeterminacy need not prevent research progress" (Haaga & Stewart, 1992b, p. 26). As long as each individual research report provides a clear operational definition for its own idiosyncratic naming of variables, the inability of the theory to distinguish between two crucial variables was not a problem (Haaga & Stewart, 1992a).

This argument is unacceptable if one's aim is to participate in the development of a coherent body of knowledge. A laissez-faire approach to the definition of crucial variables can only lead to what Staats (1991) described as "chaotic knowledge —inconsistent, nonconsensual, faddish, disorganized, unrelated, redundant— [which] is not effective scientific knowledge" (p. 910).

This brief illustration of the largely semantic basis of the separation of different types of expectations highlights an important weakness, not only of self-efficacy theory, but of the many cognitive theories that propose the interaction of beliefs and expectations as important causes of observable behavior but fail to provide adequate means of assessing them. Staddon (1984) argued that Bandura's descriptions of the causal links between internal variables are ill defined and give "the illusion of precision without the reality" (p. 507). This problem is certainly not unique to self-efficacy theory. Many cognitive–behavioral theories rely on undefined relations between hypothetical cognitive structures (Lee, 1987, 1993). Although they may give the impression of dealing with important variables, their lack of definitional rigor renders them less than scientific. It seems premature to reject a behavioral and empirical approach to psychology in favor of an approach characterized by vagueness and lack of scientific rigor. Again, the question arises: Are cognitive models of human behavior any advance on the previously dominant behavioral models? Are these the only two alternatives that exist?

Taking Things at Face Value. A further problem with the development of vague but attractive concepts is that data consistent with one's chosen theory are often assumed to support it, although they could equally support a range of alternative models. Freimuth (1992) suggested that the scientific integrity of a theory is often not the most important factor influencing psychologists' choice of a guiding framework but that social and personal factors may be more important. Motivation to maintain a particular view of the world may override more strictly logical concerns in evaluating evidence.

For example, a large amount of the self-efficacy literature has demonstrated that efficacy expectations correlate with observed or reported behavior (e.g., DiClemente et al., 1985; McAuley, 1993; Weinberg, Gould, Yukelson, & Jackson, 1981) or intentions (e.g., Hackett, 1985; Maddux, Sherer, & Rogers, 1982). Other studies demonstrated that efficacy expectations paralleled behavioral and emotional changes during therapy (e.g., Bandura et al., 1977; Williams, Turner, & Peer, 1985) or correlated with physiological measures (e.g., Bandura, Taylor, Williams, Mefford, & Barchas, 1985; Barrios, 1983).

Although such findings are not inconsistent with self-efficacy theory, they are equally consistent with other models. The central tenet, that efficacy expectations cause other phenomena, has not been tested. Biglan (1987) and Hawkins (1992) both argued that self-efficacy research results could equally be explained through a model which proposes that all the variables, expectations, behaviors, and physiological changes result directly from environmental events. That efficacy expectations may be moderately correlated with the other events need not necessarily mean they play any causal role (Hawkins, 1992).

In some cases, the impression that self-efficacy has a causal relationship with behavior is maintained by a failure to measure other potentially relevant variables. Bozoian, Rejeski, and McAuley (1994), for example, found that self-efficacy relating to exercise predicted mood enhancement following exercise. The assumption that efficacy somehow caused the mood enhancement is maintained by the fact that the researchers failed to measure variables such as experience with exercise or social reinforcement for involvement in exercise.

In a similar vein, Pajares and Miller (1995) investigated mathematics self-efficacy and concluded that efficacy level was specific to the task: Efficacy for problem solving predicted problem solving, whereas efficacy for success in mathematics predicted choice of a mathematics major. Although these findings appear to support the notion of a highly specific efficacy variable as a contributor to academic success, the authors failed to collect data on other relevant variables, such as previous performance in mathematics. Again, such a study cannot lead to any conclusions about the causes of academic success.

Other research does not make this mistake. Kaplan, Ries, Prewitt, and Eakin (1994) found self-efficacy to predict survival among patients suffering from chronic obstructive pulmonary diseases but noted that self-efficacy did not add to the variance explained by disease-related physiological measures. This finding suggests that self-efficacy might be better seen as a reflection of the actual physical cause of survival among this group.

Tryon (1982) argued that a reasonable concordance between self-efficacy and behavior may be explained if one assumes that most people in Western societies have a history of social reinforcement for consistency between verbal reports and behavior. Thus, people tend to respond to questionnaires in ways likely to be consistent with their later behavior, but the verbal reports may not reflect a causal mechanism. The wish for consistency between cognitive variables and actual behavior may be learned; this hypothesis is supported by cross-cultural research. Under some conditions, for example, Japanese respondents seem to make no such assumption about a necessary or desirable relation between self-report and behavior (Kashima, Siegal, Tanaka, & Kashima, 1992).

Wilkins (1986) put the more general argument that expectancies of any kind were reflections of previous behavior and not causes of subsequent actions. When people are asked what they expect to do next, their response is largely determined by what they did last. This is consistent with at least some self-efficacy research, which finds previous behavior to be the best predictor of behavior (e.g., Krane, Williams, & Feltz, 1992; Lee, 1983; McAuley, 1992).

Lang (1978) made the related point that self-reports of mental processes in general may not have a veridical relationship to the actual causes of behavior, of cognition, or of emotion. A number of social–psychological theories deal with the pitfalls of accepting self-reports at face value. Self-perception theory (e.g., Bem, 1972), for example, takes the view that people's main source of information about their motives and beliefs is observation of their own behaviors. Individuals concoct explanations that accord with what they see themselves doing.

Although there has been considerable debate about this issue (e.g., Smith & Miller, 1978), there is evidence (e.g., Nisbett & Wilson, 1977) that in at least some situations, individuals are unaware of the processes involved in making behavioral choices and are unable to recognize or describe the stimuli that affect their behavior. The extent to which it is possible to explain complex human behaviors without recourse to cognitive variables is discussed in chapter 6, and such arguments suggest that accepting self-reports as if they were veridical descriptions of the causes of behavior may be inappropriate.

Although proponents of social–cognitive models may be prepared to concede that models of this type have difficulties as formal theoretical models, they may argue that weaknesses in explanatory value are not important in practical terms and that if techniques derived from the theories help in alleviating distress then they are of value. However, in the following section of this chapter I argue that self-efficacy and related models are only moderately accurate in predicting human actions. Their lack of precision means that these theories eventually fail practically as well as philosophically. The view that the scientific basis of a theory is irrelevant to its practical usefulness cannot be sustained, and there are practical reasons why pragmatic psychologists should consider theoretical issues. Matters of scientific verifiability and precise measurement are not esoteric trivia for the amusement of academic psychologists but essential in practical terms as well.

SELF-EFFICACY AND RELATED THEORIES: PRACTICAL INEFFECTIVENESS

Research that examines the predictions of self-efficacy theory and related cognition-based models indicates that the success of these models is highly variable. Overall, the variables hypothesized by the models generally fail to account for most of the variance they are expected to explain. Measures of component variables hypothesized to be important are often not particularly accurate predictors of the composite cognitive variables, nor are the cognitive variables good predictors of behavior.

There have been many demonstrations that correlations between self-efficacy and behavior can be high if self-efficacy has been measured specifically and immediately prior to a straightforward, unambiguous task in a restricted environment (e.g., Biran & Wilson, 1981; Katz et al., 1983; Weinberg et al., 1981). However, well-conducted research in a number of substantive areas (e.g., Altmaier, Russell, Kao, Lehmann, & Weinstein, 1993; Luzzo, 1993; Martocchio, 1994) has failed to find any relation between self-efficacy and behavior. Over the longer term and in less controlled settings the predictive accuracy of self-efficacy is generally very low (e.g., Condiotte & Lichtenstein, 1981; DiClemente, 1981). Norman (1991), failing to find links between social learning theory variables and attendance for cancer screening, concluded that "the amount of variance explained was small, thus calling into question the utility of social learning theory in the prediction of preventive health behaviors" (Norman, 1991, p. 231).

Many publications have reported statistically significant but practically trivial relations between self-efficacy and related behavior. For example, Sadri and Robertson (1993), reviewing self-efficacy-based research on work behavior, conducted a meta-analysis of 21 studies. They found overall adjusted correlations of .4 between self-efficacy and performance, and of .34 between self-efficacy and behavioral choice. These correlations, although statistically significant, suggested that more than 80% of the variance in work-related behaviors was not predictable from self-efficacy.

Statistically significant but trivial correlations around .3 to .4, or significant percentages of variance (measured as r^2 or multiple r^2) between .1 and .2, have been commonly reported in research on smoking cessation (Garcia & Schmitz, 1990), performance on fitness tests (McAuley, 1992), and participation in exercise programs (e.g., DuCharme & Brawley, 1995; Dzewaltowski et al., 1990; Poag & McAuley, 1992).

Exclusive concentration on cognitive variables suggests that important influences on behavior may be ignored. For example, a meta-analytic review of self-efficacy research dealing with academic performance (Multon, Brown, & Lent, 1991) found a mean effect size of 0.38. The results showed enormous heterogeneity, which the reviewers were unable to attribute to research-specific factors such as differences in designs, populations, or measuring techniques. Such findings suggest that the variables responsible for this high degree of between-study variability are not ones currently being considered.

Other, theoretically less central variables such as the opinions of others (Lee, 1982), previous behavior (Feltz & Mugno, 1983; Lee, 1983), other people's previous behavior (Parker, 1994), and the sex (Betz & Hackett, 1981; Lauver & Jones, 1991) and ethnicity (Lauver & Jones, 1991) of the respondent have been found to be better predictors of behavior than the supposedly causal measures of self-efficacy. Self-efficacy is rarely as good a predictor as are observable characteristics or reports of previous behavior.

For example, McAuley (1993), in a study of physical activity in older adults, found that self-efficacy had a significant, although moderate, correlation with reported behavior but that measures of fitness and reports of previous exercise behavior were better predictors of the target behavior. Similarly, Sharpe and Connell (1992) found self-efficacy to be one of many variables significantly associated with intention to become involved in a physical activity program; however, the only predictor of actual participation one year later was reported frequency of exercise at baseline. A reasonable conclusion might be that behavior is best predicted from behavior, with self-efficacy a distorted, somewhat unreliable reflection of the respondent's recall of that behavior.

In other research, when correlations between cognition and behavior are found, they are not always explicable in terms of the theory. For example, in an efficacy-oriented study of participants in an exercise program,

McAuley, Courneya, and Lettunich (1991) found that their highest correlation ($r = .50$) was between self-efficacy for sit-ups and actual performance on a bicycle ergometer. If research finds moderate correlations between efficacy and behavior in situations such as this, in which there can be no possible causal relation, it is clear that similar correlations between efficacy and related behavior need not indicate an underlying causal relation either (Baer et al., 1986).

There is evidence for a lack of strong and consistent relations among variables within other theories as well. Variable and often weak support for hypothesized relationships seems common in research using the theory of reasoned action and the associated theory of planned behavior. A meta-analytic review of research using the theory of reasoned action (Sheppard, Hartwick, & Warshaw, 1988) examined the relations between intentions and behaviors and the relations between component beliefs (i.e., attitudes and subjective norms) and intentions. The overall adjusted correlation between intention and behavior was .53, somewhat better than research with self-efficacy theory but still a modest level of concordance. The correlation between component beliefs and intentions averaged .66, again indicating that the majority of the variance was not explicable by the theoretically relevant variables.

Sheppard et al. (1988) pointed out that the theory of reasoned action is hypothesized to predict behavior only in certain circumstances. The target behavior must be under the subject's volitional control; the subject must have all relevant information; this information must not change between measurement of the intention and observation of the behavior; and the target behavior should not involve a choice between options of similar valence, such as selecting one activity over another, equally favored choice. However, their analysis indicated that research that does not adhere to these limitations finds relations between the variables that are not much smaller than those obtained with research that complies with theoretical constraints. Choices were predicted just as well as nonchoice behaviors, despite the fact that the theory explicitly excludes them. Intentions predicted the achievement of uncontrollable goals almost as well as they predicted the performance of behaviors under direct volitional control, despite the fact that the theory states it will not hold up under these circumstances.

Although Sheppard et al. (1988) interpreted these findings as indicating the value and robustness of the theory of reasoned action, it is equally arguable that these results suggest that correlations obtained between theory of reasoned action variables may not be the result of causal relations. If the cognitive variables predict outcomes in situations in which no causal relation is hypothesized, the best explanation is that social reinforcement may encourage consistency between verbal reports and behavior (Tryon, 1982). If this explanation holds in situations that the theory of reasoned action is not designed to cover, it is logical to accept that it may be an alternative explanation for those results covered by the theory of reasoned action.

Of course, some research has found strong relations, both between component variables and intention and between intention and behavior. For example, Loken and Fishbein (1980) found component variables to predict 85% of the variance in intention to have a child in the next 3 years, and Ajzen and Fishbein (1970) found intentions to account for 92% of the variance in behavior when the topic was deciding whether or not to have an abortion. However, Bagozzi (1981) found component variables to account for only 8% of the variance in intentions to donate blood, and Warshaw, Calantone, and Joyce (1986) found intentions to account for 9% of blood-donating behavior.

Godin (1993) reviewed 21 studies that applied this theory to exercise behavior. The percentage of variance in intention accounted for by component beliefs and intention ranged from 7% to 59%. The relation between intention and actual behavior was similarly varied, with variance explained ranging from 3% to 67%. The theory offers no explanation for these discrepant results. Why should it work only some of the time?

Sheppard et al. (1988) argued that minor modifications of the theory, in particular dealing with the prediction of goals and other outcomes not under the complete volitional control of the individual, could improve accuracy. The theory of planned behavior (e.g., Ajzen & Madden, 1986) was derived from the theory of reasoned action specifically to deal with the issue of volitional control. It incorporates a measure of perceived control into the existing theory of reasoned action model. However, a theoretical review (Ajzen, 1991) that examined research using this model again revealed no consistent improvement in predictive accuracy over that of the theory of reasoned action. Correlations with behavior ranged from .18 to .84 for intentions and .11 to .76 for perceived control. Regressions combining perceived control and intentions to predict behavior produced multiple correlations ranging from .23 to .84. Godin (1993), reviewing physical activity research, found that the addition of theory of planned behavior variables to the theory of reasoned action added a mean of 8% to the variance explained. Also in the area of physical activity, Norman and Smith (1995) found that previous behavior was a better predictor than any combination of the theory of planned behavior variables.

Using the health belief model and theory of planned behavior to predict attendance at health check-ups, Norman and Conner (1993) found relations between theoretically relevant variables and attendance at screening. However, they found that these relations were completely different for those who received letters including specific appointment times and for those who received letters asking them to arrange their own appointments. If such minor procedural details can completely change the relations between cognitive variables and behavior, it is clear that there is a need to expand beyond cognition and to take environmental and systemic factors into account.

Why do the theories only seem to work some of the time? The theories themselves offer no suggestions. In chapter 3, I examine this question in detail; systematic research in this area is needed if these and similar models are to be of any practical use. An understanding of the circumstances in which their predictions will be upheld and those in which they will not could only result in a more detailed and practical understanding of the possible relations between cognitions and behavior.

Failures to predict behavior may have any of a number of explanations. They may result from measurement problems, from the possibility that the relations hypothesized by the models do not exist, from the possibility that these models apply only to some behaviors or some groups of people, or from combinations of these factors. An alternative hypothesis, however, is that this failure to predict behavior to any useful extent may result from the posited variables having no relevance to behavior at all. The small to moderate effects obtained may result from a socially reinforced tendency among respondents to demonstrate some consistency in their attitudes and behaviors (Sherman, 1980; Tryon, 1982). There is no need to hypothesize a causal link; there is no need to hypothesize, indeed, that the cognitive variables exist in any meaningful sense at all.

CONCLUSION

The arguments presented in this chapter are not simply scientific purist ones; I have used contemporary examples to show that there are good practical reasons why unscientific theories will eventually fail practically. They make no clear distinctions between various cognitions, nor do they provide any clear model of the relations between these cognitions and observable antecedents and consequences. However, they declare that cognitions cause behavior and that in order to understand human action we need to investigate cognitions.

Practically they break down, and their practical limitations are due to their scientific failings. My argument is that self-efficacy theory and other similar theories do not aid our understanding of human behavior. At the level of theoretical explanation, the statement that people behave in certain ways because of their efficacy expectations is not testable. At the level of practical techniques, this hypothesis is not useful.

Bandura's self-efficacy theory, like the other social–cognitive frameworks, is a vague descriptive model, not an explanatory theory. It provides clinicians and researchers with a nonscientific framework that names, in metaphorical terms, a hypothetical process by which behavior might result from current cognitive influences. Although it sounds sensible, there are other explanations for the research findings supposedly supporting this model.

The main practical weakness of this and similar theories is the inability to make precise predictions. The undefinable nature of the processes assumed to be involved means that there is no clear relation between observable inputs and observable results. Thus, precise predictions cannot be made, and crucial tests of the theories are impossible. This is not simply an academic purist point of view, but one that must be considered if practical and useful advances in psychological techniques are to be made. The following chapter is a discussion of whether social–cognitive models such as self-efficacy theory could ever be improved to the extent that testable and potentially falsifiable hypotheses could be derived from them. After that, I examine possibilities for the development of alternative models for the prediction and explanation of human action.

Chapter 3

Setting Limits: Improving
the Existing Cognitive Models

...generalization across contextual variables is inevitably in error. That is, there must be conditions, among the infinity of unexamined contextual variations, under which the result does not hold.
—Greenwald, Pratkanis, Leippe, & Baumgardner (1986, p. 221)

Are cognitive theories of human behavior, completely wrong? Surely, the effort expended by intelligent people around the world on the measurement of hypothetical cognitive variables, the collection and analysis of data, the writing of books and papers, submission, reviewing, revising, editing, and all the activity and expense that go into the publication of a sizeable literature would not be carried on if cognitive theories were so self-evidently a waste of time. I have no wish to deny the ability and the dedication to the understanding of personal and social processes that is demonstrated in the field. I do, however, argue that, interesting though the theories are, a very large proportion of the research based on them is of no use at all in understanding human behavior.

The problems involved in the measurement of intrinsically vague, poorly defined variables are challenging, and the development of research designs that address complicated and ill-defined theories requires sustained intellectual effort. My argument is not that research in this field is worthless but rather that it is less than optimal because the theoretical basis of the work is so poorly articulated. The enormous amount of effort expended could be more profitably used in refining the theories.

This chapter examines the possibility of improvements in several aspects of these theories. It may be possible that research could be used, not simply to demonstrate moderate levels of consistency with the vague common-sense hypotheses of these models but to make the models themselves more specific and thus more open to empirical examination. Such examination might then provide evidence that would enable assertions about the role of cognition in human behavior to be examined objectively.

The aim of this chapter is to consider the possibility that cognitive–behavioral theories can be developed to a point at which they will be able to predict at least some classes of behavior in at least some situations. Skinner (1990) pointed out that behaviorists have responded to an unsympathetic mainstream by developing their own separate professional organizations, journals, and terms of reference. Before endorsing this negative reaction, however, one should examine the possibility that mainstream research could begin to achieve consistency and accuracy at the descriptive level. If theories relating cognitions to behaviors were refined so that they made precise predictions, it might then be possible to debate the relevance of cognition to behavior. It might be possible, for example, to identify the types of circumstance in which particular cognitive variables are useful predictors of behavior and those in which they are not. Thus, without denying the basic problems inherent in models that require nonmaterial events to cause events in the material world (Eysenck, 1978), it might be possible to find a more limited but more useful role for these theories.

Greenwald, Pratkanis, Leippe, and Baumgardner (1986) expressed the view that blind adherence to specific theories and theory-confirming research must limit our understanding of psychological phenomena. They argued that there is too much emphasis on theory confirmation in psychology. Results consistent with a theory are accepted as evidence in support of that theory. Furthermore, as Weinstein (1993) argued, "researchers typically select one theory to test or to guide their choice of explanatory variables as if the other theories did not exist" (p. 324). This approach, when combined with the vagueness of the theories and the use of statistically significant correlations between self-reports as the only criterion for judging the existence of causal relationships, leads to a situation in which no theory stands a chance of being seriously challenged on empirical grounds. As Greenwald et al. (1986) argued, an emphasis on defining the limits and conditions under which specific theories hold up is likely to be more fruitful.

In the following sections I consider ways in which social cognitive theories might be refined and their limits explored. If progress could be made on these points, then arguments for the utility of models of this type would be strengthened. On the other hand, if the questions are not amenable to empirical investigation, then the problems identifiable in connection with social cognitive theories may be intrinsic to theories of this type. Such a conclusion seems to lead inevitably to the argument that we need a radically different way of looking at human behavior.

IMPROVING THE COGNITIVE MODELS

Describing Influences on Cognitions

Where do cognitive variables come from? Cognitions are hypothesized to be influenced by the environment and also by biological variables that are long-term and stable or temporary, such as state of health, hunger, and thirst. Experiences are filtered and interpreted on the basis of generalized schemata, consisting of broad sets of cultural values and central beliefs, themselves derived from earlier experiences (e.g., Guidano & Liotti, 1983).

However, suggesting that vicarious experiences affect levels of self-efficacy in a new situation (e.g., Bandura, 1986) or that habit strength has an effect on the probability of a behavior occurring (e.g, Triandis, 1980), without any concept of how these influences should be measured, does not provide information that allows one to make any predictions beyond those dictated by commonsense. The theories need to specify how, for example, vicarious experiences might impinge upon cognitions. A method for quantifying vicarious experiences (or whichever variable is being considered) is needed prior to the development of such models. For example, the effect that vicarious experiences have on current cognitions may be influenced by the type, frequency, and recency of the experiences as well as by the distribution of various types of related or contradictory experiences. There is no work that attempts to systematize the assessment of experiences so that it would be possible to predict the influence that a particular combination of experiences has on a particular cognition.

Some limited empirical research does examine the sources of self-efficacy. Lent, Lopez, and Bieschke (1991), examining mathematics self-efficacy in college students, attempted to assess the four classes of input named by Bandura (e.g., 1986) and to examine their relations with self-efficacy. The four sources indeed correlated with self-efficacy when they were forced into a hierarchical regression equation in the order predicted by the theory. However, the only theoretically relevant variable to add significantly to the amount of variance explained by gender (a variable that Bandura's theory fails to mention) was performance accomplishment. This concept clearly refers to previous overt behavior and is the only variable hypothesized by self-efficacy theory that is directly verifiable. Thus, although it was possible to obtain a moderately accurate prediction of mathematics self-efficacy from measurements of the four components, in fact Lent et al. (1991) could get a more accurate prediction from a knowledge of a student's gender and previous mathematics grades.

There is considerable scope for further research of this type to develop more accurate cognitive–behavioral theories. Retrospective self-reports, despite their limitations, can be used to collect information about experience relevant to a wide range of hypothesized cognitive variables. Other methods require more elaborate designs but might provide more accurate information. These include longitudinal studies of persons engaged in repeated experiences with an activity, such as learning a new motor skill. Even intervention studies in which subjects are exposed to novel experiences and the effects on target variables are assessed might be possible.

Whatever method was used, it might be possible to develop methods that allow more accurate assessment of the variables hypothesized to influence the theoretically relevant cognitions and thus allow predictions to be made about individuals' reactions in novel situations; surely, this is a basic criterion of a scientific theory, and one that current cognitive–behavioral theories do not meet. A new self-efficacy theory that incorporates a method for assessing the person's previous history and for using this information to make specific statements about the extent and type of influence that these experiences are likely to have on cognitions (or even on behavior) would be a self-efficacy theory with some scientific rigor.

Examining Relationships Among Influences on Cognitions

A logical extension of the points made above is the need to provide more precise models of how the different hypothesized influences on the theoretically central cognitions might interact. Most models assume that some sort of interaction takes place but go into no detail about the nature of these interactions. If a person has had one negative experience with a particular activity but has observed others in a range of positive experiences and has read information concerning the possible dangers of that activity, what might be the overall effect on self-efficacy? How many vicarious positive experiences, of what nature, might counteract a single, actual, negative experience? Such questions cannot be answered by self-efficacy theory, and a similar point can be made for the other models addressed in this book.

A clear-cut method is required for assessing the individual variables hypothesized to affect cognition. Following this, research examining combinations of measures might enable models to be developed to predict more precisely how a particular set of experiences, observations, verbal inputs, and other influences affects the target cognitions.

Defining the Interactions Among Cognitions

Whereas self-efficacy theory argues for a single crucial cognitive variable that determines behavior, other theories argue that external sources give rise to a number of different types of cognition, which then combine to form a cognitive outcome, which itself influences behavior. Some models (e.g., Fishbein & Ajzen, 1976) are quite specific concerning methods for establishing the precise relations, at least for closely defined behaviors in specific groups of people. There is a need to extend research of this kind to develop models that allow specific predictions to be made. The health belief model, for example, specifies a number of cognitive variables but not how they interact. The model is so vague that almost any outcome could be explained after the fact, but none could be predicted with any degree of certainty.

Some research attempts to redress this problem, but it is in its early stages. Ronis (1992), for example, argued that the health belief model and the theory of subjective expected utility could be combined, and he provided a strong argument supported by mathematical formulas. His first study examined a hypothetical disease and a hypothetical preventative action; different levels of susceptibility, severity, and benefits of action were presented to different subjects. He predicted that information on severity and susceptibility would not have direct effects on reported intention to engage in preventative action but would be mediated by information about the benefit of the action. The path analysis supported his hypothesis, to the extent that the predicted path coefficients were significantly different from zero (although not particularly large; partial correlations ranged from $r = .15$ to $r = .67$), and only one of four nonpredicted paths showed a significant relation. Clearly the model was not perfectly accurate, but this investigation did, to some extent, support his argument.

Sensitive to the problems of hypothetical situations, Ronis (1992) repeated his survey using an actual behavior, dental flossing, as well as a wider subject pool and performed a similar path analysis to that undertaken in the first study. The results were, however, nothing like those of the previous one. The best predictor of reported behavior was the measure of perceived costs (which had not been assessed in the hypothetical model, so that the two designs were not directly comparable); $r = -.24$, which, although significantly different from zero, indicated a very low correlation between the two sets of self-reports. The next highest coefficient, assessing the direct relation between perceived susceptibility and reported behavior ($r = .21$), was one specifically predicted to be nonsignificant. To summarize, the model developed and tested in the first study did not include all the variables measured in the second study, and those variables common to both studies behaved in entirely different ways in the two analyses. In general, correlations between the various classes of self-report were quite low.

This study was a rigorous piece of research that dealt with many problems —the adequacy of the measures, the appropriateness of artificial laboratory tasks, the problems of relying on student subjects, the need for more specific and sophisticated models—that plague research of this nature. It is easy for the critic to disparage poor quality research, but my point is that even a well-conducted piece of work such as this fails to produce a replicable model of the hypothetical variables and their relations.

It has been argued that (cf. Corrigan, 1990) we simply need to continue such research, using traditional statistical strategies such as multiple regression, discriminant analysis, and path analysis, and the theories will gradually but inexorably develop into accurate and complete models of human behavior. However, it may be that these approaches, with their underlying assumption that all human behavior, in all persons, is caused in a simple linear fashion by a small number of cognitions, will never be adequate to produce accurate descriptions of human behavior (Lee, 1990). It may be necessary to move beyond the traditional statistical tools and make use of the nonlinear modeling strategies now being developed in other fields (Halasz, 1995; Mandel, 1995; Schuster, 1989). Most important, it may be necessary to question the assumptions that cognition causes behavior and that cognition is the only relevant variable for psychology.

Describing Relations Between Composite Cognitions and Behavior

I have considered the difficulties of describing the environmental influences on cognitions, of discussing ways in which such influences might interact with each other, of developing models of the interactions between the cognitions that arise from this hypothetical process, and of measuring these variables. The next stage is the relation between composite cognitions, the end products of the cognitive process, and behavior.

Self-efficacy theory (e.g., Bandura, 1986) states that self-efficacy is the proximal determinant of behavior, provided the individual has "appropriate skills and adequate incentives" (Bandura, 1977, p. 194); the theory of reasoned action (e.g., Ajzen & Fishbein, 1980) that behavioral intention predicts behavior provided an appropriate environment exists for that behavior. Again what is lacking is a model that allows predictions about the situations in which these variables will optimally predict behavior and the situations in which they will be less accurate. As Mixon (1991) argued, these theories are silent on the circumstances under which people fail to do what they intend to do, despite apparently having the requisite skills and incentives. The role of other variables in these relations is totally ignored; if they are mentioned at all, these variables are simply named, and the false impression is given that they have been explained away.

Sarver (1983), in a critique of the theory of reasoned action, pointed out that whether the person has an opportunity to engage in the target behavior is never considered. The same comment can be made of the other models, which fail to deal in any coherent way with environmental constraints. Sarver (1983) pointed out that the theory of reasoned action stated that intentions do not lead to behavior if unforeseen events arise, but he considered that "a fleeting reference of this sort can hardly take the place of a sustained and systematic consideration of those factors which bear on the context of opportunity" (p. 157). In the same way, Bandura's invocation of skills and incentives as necessary conditions for self-efficacy to produce behavior is unsatisfactory.

In real life, too, people deal with more than one alternative and more than one set of beliefs (Kuhl, 1985). The theory of reasoned action and the theory of planned behavior state that such situations are outside their limits (although the theories predict behavior in these situations as well or as badly as they do in any other situation). The other theories simply ignore the possibility of competing responses.

Defining Limits

More rigorous models may also be much less general in their application. Measures of external variables and relevant cognitions that combine appropriately for some behavioral targets, some environments, or some population groups might be quite inappropriate for others. Greater specificity and a narrowed range of applicability do not reduce explanatory value. Rather, the ability to define the limits of a model is an indicator of its strength. If cognitive–behavioral models can be developed that provide accurate descriptions of behavior, even if they apply only in circumscribed situations and with a limited range of behaviors, and if one can state in advance the limits of their applicability, they will demonstrate that it is possible to develop cognitively based models that have empirical support. On the other hand, if it is not possible, even within quite narrow constraints, to develop an accurate cognitively based model for predicting behavior, cognitions may be less central to behavioral choices than is currently believed.

Behavioral Limits. The work of Ronis (1992) illustrated that models that are satisfactory for one behavior may be inappropriate for others. Will a model that predicts dental flossing also predict cheating in examinations? Are the same variables, combining in the same way, as relevant to choosing a college major as they are to choosing a marriage partner? If not, why not?

There has been little success in the development of all-encompassing models of human behavior. Perhaps it would be useful to consider strategies for grouping behaviors that might be predicted more accurately, although by more limited theories. It is possible, for example, that behaviors might be predicted in similar ways if they have been acquired in similar ways. Alternatively, activities conducted for their intrinsically rewarding properties may be predicted by different models from those conducted for indirect advantage, such as health or earning capacity. Or it may be that activities involving other people, compared to solitary activities, may alter the pattern of predictors. Consider also the length of time taken to complete the activity: writing a doctoral dissertation versus cooking a cordon bleu meal, both highly skilled and complex behaviors but one requiring persistence over many years whereas the other can be completed in a few hours.

Yet again, it may be that contingencies of reinforcement are important; negatively reinforced behaviors may be predicted in a different way from positively reinforced ones, those associated with primary reinforcers can be compared to those with secondary, those in which reinforcement is continuous and predictable contrast with those in which reinforcement is variable or thin. Consider also behaviors requiring a certain level of skill, those that must be practiced regularly, those that occur frequently versus those that are carried out on rare occasions. A list of this nature has no limits because there is no externally verifiable or generally accepted method for classifying behaviors. It is possible, however, that such a method might provide a valuable basis for the development of models that seriously and rigorously considered the relation between aspects of the behavior under investigation and aspects of models for that behavior's prediction.

Demographic Limits. It is also quite probable that models that predict behavior accurately in particular demographic and cultural groups may not work in others. The cognitive variables hypothesized by the theories under discussion are conceived as the product of experience. When do they develop? Do they become more or less complex as the years go by? Are there cultural differences? There is very little research exploring demographic factors and their possible relation with theoretically relevant variables. Gender (e.g., Lent et al., 1991) and ethnicity (e.g., Heine &

Lehman, 1995; Lauver & Jones, 1991; Rogoff & Chavajay, 1995) have been shown to be associated with differences in cognitive variables, but is it possible that the relations between cognitive variables are different for different ethnic and demographic groups? People from Asian cultures, for example, are often considered to be more collectivist than people of European origin (Heine & Lehman, 1995; Spence, 1985). Might it be that, for persons with such a perspective, vicarious observation and verbal information might be more, not less, influential than individual performance accomplishments? The possibility that the hypothesized relations between imaginary variables are specific to people with particular cultural or educational experiences and inappropriate for others has not been explored, but it is clearly important if these theories are to reflect our understanding of human diversity.

CONCLUSION

Not only have social and cognitive psychology not taken the questions raised in this chapter seriously, but currently popular models of human behavior are incapable of making a serious contribution to answering them. In the next chapter, I examine evidence that challenges the core assumption of these theories, the assumption that all human behavior, or at least all interesting human behavior, is caused by cognition. Evidence from a number of areas of psychology is used to argue that cognition may not be as central to human behavior as contemporary cognitive–behavioral theories argue.

Chapter 4

Thinking Makes It So: The Presumption That Cognition Causes Everything

> *... it is likely that other non-cognitive variables are important in the determination of ... behaviour. As they stand, most of the currently employed models are not placed in a wider context, and as a result do not consider broader social, economic and environmental influences on behaviour ... these factors are only seen to have an indirect influence on behaviour through their effect on an individual's cognitions.*
>
> —Norman and Conner (1993, p. 459)

It is of course necessary for scientific fields to have working assumptions about their subject matter. Theories act as simplified models of reality, which provide a basis on which ideas can be explored (Chalmers, 1982). Human activity is too complex for a grand unified theory to spring fully formed into existence. Our theories are partial and necessarily incomplete, and it may be that the best one can hope for is that a continual process of refinement will gradually expand their boundaries and increase their explanatory power; it may be ignorant or naive to expect more.

However, although working assumptions are necessary, they are no more than assumptions, untested or even untestable (Skinner, 1989). The fundamental question that this book deals with is whether thought actually directs human action. Applied and social psychology rest on the assumption that the answer to this question is so obviously "yes" that there is no point in asking it. Psychology assumes that studying cognition is the only legitimate way to understand human behavior (Bolton, 1991). The value of this assumption is that it simplifies the enormous task of understanding why human beings behave the way they do; the task, still dauntingly huge and complex but at least approachable, becomes that of assessing thoughts and searching for lawful relationships among thoughts and between thoughts and behavior.

The theories I discuss in this book are based on the untested assumption that people's actions and emotions are determined by cognitive factors such as attitudes, attributions, and locus of control. Therefore, although physiology, biochemistry, behavior, and environment are relevant, in the final analysis human nature can only be understood when cognitions, the proximal causes of behavior, are understood (Campbell, 1970). As Kuhl and Beckmann (1985) put it, "understanding human cognition seems the first logical step towards an explanation of human behavior" (p. 1). It appears immediately obvious that thinking controls action, but the immediate obviousness of a point of view is not necessarily related to truth or to utility (Skinner, 1990).

A major problem with cognition-centered models of human action is that they are based on a confusion between the way human beings appear from the inside to work and the way in which they actually work. In other fields, scientists accept that the way things look from a human perspective and the way they actually are need not be the same. We recognize that the world is not flat, even though it looks flat from where we stand. We recognize that the stars are enormous fiery balls of gas, even though they look like small cold points of light to us. In a similar way, we may need to explore the possibility that human action works differently from the way that it feels.

From the inside, it feels very much as if what we think controls what we do and how we feel. My argument is that this feeling, however strong, is not an adequate basis for a scientific model of human behavior. Cognition is not necessarily a veridical cause of behavior (e.g., Skinner, 1990), but perhaps it is a result of that behavior or an irrelevant side effect of behavior and physiology. This relates closely to major philosophical questions concerning the nature of mind and brain, the nature of causality, and the possibility that nonphysical events have effects in a material world. It has been stressed by a number of theorists (e.g., Eysenck, 1978; Quine, 1989) that cognitions are metaphorical labels for highly complex physiological and neurochemical processes that we are yet to understand and that cognitive models do not explain anything at a basic scientific level, but exist only as loose descriptions of processes we do not understand.

Cognitions, it is argued (e.g., Meichenbaum, 1993), are metaphors, but they are useful and necessary metaphors because our limited understanding of basic processes prevents us from describing human behavior in more basic terms. However, this level of explanation can be seen as better than none at all. Kimble (1989), for example, held that a radical science of behavior might satisfy the positivists but, in its current form, it leaves out everything that the psychologist sets out to understand, whereas Munro (1992) argued that models at different levels of analysis or explanation should not be viewed in a hierarchy of value, a series of successively better approximations to absolute truth, but that each level had its own unique value in dealing with its own set of phenomena.

The central problem with arguments of this kind is that, if one is content with a metaphorical description of imaginary predictors of activity, then, given the theoretical problems outlined in the earlier chapters, it is impossible for the field of psychology to develop in a structured way. The failure of social cognitive models to produce workable descriptions of human activity, together with their lack of a scientific basis, are cause for rejecting these theories in favor of development of behavioral and alternative materialistic models of human behavior (e.g., Ledwidge, 1978; Lee, 1990; Skinner, 1977, 1990), while paying more attention to broader contextual and environmental influences on behavior (Morris, 1988; Prilleltensky, 1989).

The main focus of this chapter is to examine critically the view that conscious, or at least reportable, cognitions control human emotional experience. The assumption that cognition causes overt behaviors is examined in chapters 5 and 6, in which some alternative models are explored, but this chapter focuses on emotion. Although contemporary theories in clinical psychology have emphasized the role of cognition in the development (e.g., Ellis, 1987, 1993) or maintenance (Beck, 1991) of negative emotions, evidence from other research areas within psychology suggests that this is by no means the only legitimate view.

THE PRIMACY OF COGNITION IN EMOTIONAL EXPERIENCE: CONTRADICTORY EVIDENCE

The James–Lange model, the view that emotion arises from a cognitive explanation of generalized arousal, which forms the basis of many contemporary theories, is no longer tenable (cf. Reisenzein, 1984). Differential-emotions theories (e.g., Izard, 1977), which have their basis in evidence for different physiological processes underlying different emotions, have gained widespread acceptance within physiological psychology, and an understanding of the underlying neural basis must constrain and inform our models of emotion (LeDoux, 1995).

Despite this, the contemporary view among clinical psychologists is still that negative affect arises as a result of cognitions, particularly as a result of faulty cognitive interpretation of circumstances (e.g., Ellis, 1984). An enormous amount of literature exists dealing with depressives' cognitions, which are indeed frequently negative (Hollon & Beck, 1979), although not necessarily incorrect (Alloy & Abramson, 1979). For example, depressed people tend to behave in ways that elicit negative social responses from other people (Howes & Hokanson, 1979) and thus a feeling of rejection need not be inaccurate.

Many well-controlled studies using cognitive methods to treat dysfunctional emotions have shown positive results (Beck, 1993), although the question of whether cognitive change is the mechanism by which improvements occur remains open (Latimer & Sweet, 1984; Oei, Hansen, & Miller, 1993), and there is evidence to indicate that, at least with some subject groups, these methods are no better than credible placebos (Kuiper & MacDonald, 1983). The consensus among reviewers has been that the effectiveness of cognitive procedures, with all behavioral components excluded, has not been convincingly demonstrated (Beidel & Turner, 1986; Latimer & Sweet, 1984). Furthermore, there is some evidence (e.g., Newman, Hofmann, Trabert, Roth, & Taylor, 1994) to suggest that purely behavioral methods are not only successful in changing behavior but also are as effective as cognitive methods in changing levels of subjective distress. Feske and Chambless (1995) concluded, on the basis of a meta-analysis of treatments for social phobia, that they had "found no evidence for the proposed superiority of CBT over exposure on measures of cognitive symptoms" (p. 713).

The cognitive theory of depression proposed by Beck (e.g., 1991) is the most well-articulated explanation of the most frequently occurring emotional problem in Western society. However, a recent review of its value, not as a therapeutic metaphor but as a theoretical explanation of depression (Haaga, Dyck, & Ernst, 1991), concluded that there was "little convincing support for the causal hypotheses of cognitive theory" (p. 231). Although therapeutic results are generally positive, there are some major problems with the theory qua theory.

Their empirical review supported Beck's arguments that depressives' cognitions were characterized by negativity and that negative cognitions were common to all classes of depression, but Haaga et al. (1991) found less empirical support for other central principles of the theory. There was little evidence that depressive thoughts were exclusively negative, or even that negative thoughts were a necessary component of depression. There is also little evidence that severity of depressive thoughts will correlate with severity of other symptoms, as Beck proposed they should, except that high levels of reported "hopelessness," one of a number of categories of depressive thought, are predictive of suicide.

The proposed automatic character of negative thoughts in depression had never been tested, according to Haaga et al. (1991), who also described the concept of the cognitive triad (i.e., negative views about the self, the world, and the future) as conceptually confused, with the three categories overlapping and the questionnaires designed to assess the three failing to distinguish clearly between them. The issue of cognitive distortion, the view that depressed people see the world in a systematically biased way, is an aspect of many other theories besides Beck's and is considered independently in chapter 7, which deals with the issues of rationality and bias in human thought more generally.

Beck (1991) argued that depression is caused when depressogenic schemata arise in individuals with particular personality types. However, Haaga et al. (1991) also found no evidence that people who develop depression could be identified a priori on the basis of any distinct personality type or particular classes of schemata.

Beck's hypothesis that particular thought content is specific to depressives can also be challenged. A recent analog study (Ambrose & Rholes, 1993) measured symptoms of depression and anxiety, as well as frequency of thoughts associated with depression and with anxiety, in normal adolescents. Controlling for anxiety symptoms and anxiety-related thoughts, the relation of depressive thoughts to depressive symptoms, although statistically significant, was minuscule, contributing 6.2% of the variance. Depressive thoughts were related as closely to symptoms of anxiety as they were to symptoms of depression, suggesting that they are by no means specific to depression and need not necessarily cause depression.

Thus, although this model is the best of the cognition-centered views of dysfunctional emotion, with decades of research effort behind it (see, for example, Beck, 1963, as well as Beck's 1991 review of 30 years of research on depression and his 1993 review of the theory's application to other psychological problems), it does not measure up well as an explanatory model. It may be that models that focus exclusively on cognition in attempting to understand emotion are missing something important.

Arguments Against the Primacy of Cognition

Against the moderate success of cognitive behavioral treatments for affective disorders must be set the powerful arguments, summarized by Zajonc (1980, 1984), against the assumption that cognition causes affect. Zajonc reviewed evidence that affective judgments persist without cognitive recognition of the object being judged; that recognizable affective responses occur in organisms that have no recognizable cognition, such as newborn infants and neurologically unsophisticated species; and that affective judgments are often uncorrelated with cognitive variables. Zajonc concluded that the experience of emotion occurs prior to cognition, rather than the other way around.

Rachman (1980) argued along similar lines but from a therapeutic perspective when he proposed the concept of emotional processing. Rachman argued that behavior therapy was effective in dealing with disorders having a strong affective component, such as phobias, because it provided a safe and structured setting for processing emotional experiences until they were no longer disruptive to behavior. Therapy, he suggested, was a process by which emotions lost their disruptive quality and came to play a positive role in healthy functioning (Rachman, 1984). According to this approach, cognitive changes were reflections of the change process rather than its cause.

The extensive literature on the influences of affect and mood on memory (e.g., Blaney, 1986) makes it clear that individuals' cognitions are strongly influenced by their moods. Bower (1981) concluded from his own experimental work that "emotion powerfully influenced such cognitive processes as free associations, imaginative fantasies, social perceptions, and snap judgments about others' personalities" (p. 129).

Early research on the influence of emotion on cognition emphasized the disruptive effects of feelings, particularly on analytical reasoning (Schwarz & Bless, 1991). Such research seemed to be based on the assumption that emotional reactions were somehow wrong, or at least definitely inferior to rational thought. However, the relationship seems to be more complex than that. Schwarz and Bless (1991) argued that affective state provides information that modifies cognitive style; evidence suggests that negative moods tend to lead to more analytical reasoning, whereas good moods produce a more creative, inferential approach. In a similar vein, Petty, Gleicher, and Baker (1991) argued that affect influenced attitudes by motivating the person to think about the subject and by influencing the types of thought as well as by influencing information processing.

To propose a unidirectional effect of cognition on affect is simply not tenable. It follows that to propose that all emotional states arise from cognitive appraisal and thus that emotional dysfunction can only be treated by altering cognition is an oversimplification of a complex process and is unlikely to produce optimal therapeutic strategies.

Some recent developments in behavioral and cognitive–behavioral theory emphasize complex reciprocal interactions between behavior, cognition, and affect. Zajonc (1980) argued that there may be two separate but partially dependent mental systems, affective and cognitive, responsible respectively for "preferenda" and for "discriminanda," and underlain by separate but interacting physiological processes.

Although Zajonc's approach attempted to integrate a large amount of empirical evidence from a range of sources, it still begged the question of what exactly is meant by information processing. Computer metaphors of human behavior have gained great popularity in recent years, and it is easy to forget that "people and machines do not have the same attributes" (Locke, 1994, p. 367) and are not comparable except at a trivial level. Information processing is a metaphorical label for a process, rather than an explanation of how it occurs (Costall, 1991).

Rachman (1981) followed Zajonc's original argument with a description of some implications of a model that involves affect as more than the outcome of a dysfunctional cognitive process. He proposed that the phenomenon of desynchrony (Rachman & Hodgson, 1974) between behavior, cognition, and affect could be explained by Zajonc's model. Zajonc's theoretical arguments provided a rationale for the therapist to select a treatment focused on the most prominently affected of the three components, rather than always, necessarily, focusing on cognitive change.

Rachman suggested that the model also provided an explanation for the observation that certain people (e.g., phobics) continue to behave abnormally even when they recognize that their actions are irrational, an observation that cognitive theories are unable to explain. More generally, it may provide an explanation for the intransigence of some emotional problems in the face of methods that focus on cognitive change. It may be inappropriate to deal with problems that are basically emotional through a focus on cognitive change.

If affect is a partially independent system and not a product of cognition, clinical psychology should seek to develop more direct techniques of assessing and modifying affect. Rachman (1984) suggested a number of objectively observable or unambiguously reportable indices of emotional processing, including obsessive activities, physiological measures, reports of disturbing dreams, and insomnia. The concept of emotional processing, Rachman suggested, could be used to explain why a variety of behavioral techniques have similar fear-reducing effects.

Thus, Rachman's emotional-processing concept aimed to provide an explanation of therapeutic change that unified a range of different therapeutic strategies by identifying a common emotional process by which change occurred, in much the same way as Bandura's (1977) concept of self-efficacy attempted to identify a common cognitive process. It is interesting to note the differing extent to which these two concepts have been taken up by psychologists across research and clinical areas and to speculate as to why the cognitive concept has been accepted so much more readily than the emotional one.

This is not to say that Rachman's arguments have been ignored. A small amount of research (e.g., Clark, 1983; Eifert, 1985) has focused on the use of music to alter affective states, with some preliminary success. However, a problem with this approach is that it relies on the assumption that music is processed emotionally and not cognitively. The current state of our theoretical and empirical understanding of affect, cognition, and the difference between them does not allow for this assumption to be tested.

Indeed, at a more basic level, the assumption that affect and cognition are different from each other and can be influenced independently of each other is questionable. Although this point is by no means new (Duffy, 1934), it is worthy of repetition because of the apparent ease with which people can assume that, because we have distinct terms for affect and cognition, they must be two separate phenomena.

Arguments for the Interdependency of Cognition and Affect

A number of authors have questioned the usefulness of treating emotion and cognition as separate systems. Zajonc and Markus (1984) argued that both thoughts and feelings are represented within the organism in a number of different ways. This accords with the view that emotions are multidimensional response syndromes with affective, cognitive, behavioral, and physiological components (Reisenzein, 1984). The concept of physical involvement in emotion is neither new nor contentious (see, for example, McGuigan, 1970). Zajonc's argument, however, is not the older, reductionist one that the physical involvement defines and explains the cognitive or emotional event (e.g., Fryer, 1941) but that both affect and cognition are represented by a number of systems that operate in loose parallel. He termed the mental experience and subjective report "soft representations" and the objectively measurable physical events "hard representations" of processes occurring simultaneously in a number of channels and argued that this view rendered irrelevant the notion of distinguishing between cognitions and emotions. Zajonc did not suggest that the soft representations were necessarily illusory or epiphenomenal, merely that they could not be measured objectively. Thus, he argued for a focus on the measurement of physical and physiological processes and overt behaviors as an approach to understanding affect. More recently, Zajonc, Murphy, and Inglehart (1989) argued for a role of vascular processes in the development of emotional state and linked this to the effects of facial expression on reported emotion.

The interdependence of emotion and cognition has been taken a step further. It has been argued that it is useful to regard affect and cognition not as fundamentally different events but as different aspects of the same thing. To use Zajonc's terminology, this phenomenon has both hard and soft components, with affect and cognition being soft representations of events simultaneously occurring physiologically. Several authors have suggested that cognitions and emotions are not separate mental events but rather different dimensions of the same phenomenon (Greenberg & Safran, 1984; Lee, 1987; Zajonc & Markus, 1984). Greenberg and Safran (1984) have distinguished between "hot" and "cold" cognition, with hot cognition including both facts and feelings about those facts, and cold being cognition having no emotional component. From this perspective, the question of which is prior to the other becomes meaningless.

Nonscientific Models of Affect

In evaluating these contributions to our understanding of cognition and affect, it is important to note that simply acknowledging the insufficiency of an assumption of unidirectional causation is not in itself sufficient for a model to be an improvement on the cognition-centered ones. Some of the newer models of emotion are more useful than others. The primary distinguishing feature of those likely to be productive at theoretical, empirical, and practical levels is an emphasis on the objectively measurable. Some recently described models that appear to take noncognitive aspects of emotion into account suffer from the problems discussed earlier with reference to cognition: They describe complex interactions between hypothetical mediating variables, unobservable both in practice and in principle.

Learning as Affect: Evaluative Conditioning.   Levey and Martin (1983a) argued for an evaluative conditioning model of learning, in which emotion takes the place of thought as the mechanism by which behavior is changed. They suggested that classical conditioning involved the transfer of an emotional evaluation from the UCS to the CS. The qualities they ascribed to evaluative responses were similar to those Zajonc ascribed to emotional responses, and Levey and Martin (1983a) drew on Zajonc's arguments, among others, to support their model. However, it is difficult to see the value of the evaluative conditioning model. The major problem is one of definition. As Levey and Martin (1983a) described it, the evaluative response is neither an observable response nor a reportable internal event. Rather, it is the cause of these events, observable only indirectly through its effects on them.

Central to the evaluative conditioning model is the argument that behavior can be changed only by changing the evaluative response. However, the evaluative response cannot be observed, only inferred from behavior. This model simply replaces unobservable cognitions with unobservable emotional responses. It postulates an entity that can only be inferred through its products, and there is no independent measure of its existence.

Levey and Martin (1983b) argued further that re-emergence of maladaptive behavior following therapy was the result of a failure to extinguish the evaluative response completely. Again, this argument suffers from circularity, as there appears to be no way one could tell, except by observing behavior, that the evaluative response had re-emerged and thus that it had not completely disappeared in the first place. The postulation of an evaluative response without the provision of any independent means of measuring it is exactly the same type of nonscientific hypothesising that has been criticized in earlier chapters with reference to cognitive –behavioral models of human emotional dysfunction.

Rachman's (1980) emotional processing model suggests a number of tests, such as exposure to the distressing situation, to assess the extent of processing. Although one may question what exactly is meant by emotional processing, empirical verification is possible at least on this level. Levey and Martin's (1983a) concept cannot be tested in this way. As they described it, the evaluative response cannot be measured objectively. However, they suggested a physiological basis to the evaluative response. They did not define the evaluative response scientifically (i.e., in such a way that we would be able to tell whether or not it had occurred), but they argued that this was not, in principle, impossible.

Affective States as Schemata.   A number of theorists (e.g., Greenberg & Safran, 1984; Guidano & Liotti, 1983; Kuiper & MacDonald, 1983) have used information-processing theories to develop cognitive models of affect. They argued that affect is a synthetic process that interacts with, rather than precedes, cognition. Their models of affect derived from Leventhal's three-stage perceptual–motor structure (e.g., Leventhal & Mosbach, 1982), which proposes a reciprocal interaction among three systems to produce the initial emotional response. Facial–motor feedback interacts with the schematic emotion memory and with a conceptual system incorporating general belief structures.

This complex process is described as occurring at a preconscious level, and thus those parts not directly involved with the facial –motor mechanism are not open to observation or analysis. The difficulty caused by a lack of empirical falsifiability is even more of a concern with these models than with the evaluative conditioning model and the cognitive–behavioral models. The schema-based models rely for their explanatory power on processes that are by definition unobservable.

With the other models, there is certainly a need to refine the theories so that objective observations may be used to test specific hypotheses. With the schema models, however, the crucial variables are unobservable in principle. Although these models may appear to provide an understanding of complex emotional processes, this understanding is illusory. Models that rely on complex but undefined interactions between structures unobservable both in theory and in practice, even indirectly through self-report, are of no explanatory value.

Physiological Events as Causal Elements

A more objective method is needed if unambiguous assessment, either of hypothetical cognitive variables or of emotions, is to become possible (Lee, 1987). The problems inherent in a reliance on self-report inventories to measure hypothetical variables have already been discussed, and the more complex the model, the more difficult the conversion of hypothetical constructs into usable questions (Mullen et al., 1987).

The use of physiological measures to infer affective and cognitive processes may be a useful way of exploring these relationships (e.g., Ekman, Levenson, & Friesen, 1983; Fridlund, Schwartz, & Fowler, 1984; Winton, Putnam, & Krauss, 1984). Inferences of this nature produce a set of new problems of interpretation (e.g., Cacioppo & Tassinary, 1990), but the use of objective measures at least reduces one source of error.

It would be incorrect to contend that current psychophysiological knowledge can explain the phenomena associated with emotional experience. However, recent developments in the measurement and recording of physiological processes and microbehaviors are beginning to allow objective measurement in areas that were previously not available for empirical observation. It is possible that eventually theories will be developed that are as general as the current cognitive ones while still having a basis in the objectively measurable. Psychophysiology, for example, may be developing the potential to allow us to understand emotional events; it may be that future developments in behavioral theory and technique will require a stronger focus on the assessment of physiological events.

Psychophysiological work in the field of the expression and communication of emotion appears to render untenable the notion that emotions are totally unobservable internal processes as well as the view that they always arise subsequent to and as a consequence of cognitions. For example, distinguishable patterns of tension and relaxation in facial muscles have been reliably associated with self-reports of various affective states (e.g., Ekman et al., 1983; Fridlund et al., 1984; Winton et al., 1984). This provides empirical support for differential emotions theories (e.g., Izard, 1977). Schwartz and his colleagues (Schwartz, Fair, Salt, Mandel, & Klerman, 1976; Schwartz, Fair, Mandel, Salt, Mieske, & Klerman, 1978) found distinguishable patterns of muscle activity across emotions in both depressed and nondepressed subjects, and the two subject groups showed significantly different patterns, suggesting the potential for assessing depressive states, at least in part, through a wider range of physiological measures. Chabrol, Barrere, Guell, and Moron (1986) showed the blood flow in the prefrontal cerebral region to be lower for clinically depressed than for nondepressed subjects; this difference was diminished when the depression was controlled by medication. Zajonc et al. (1989) argued that facial expressions may influence cerebral blood flow, which in turn may affect the release of neurotransmitters, all without any cognitive involvement at all.

Facial muscle activity has traditionally been viewed as an *expression*, an outward manifestation of a subjective experience. However, several researchers indicate that the relation between facial muscle activity and subjective emotion appears to be a reciprocal one. Adelman and Zajonc (1989) concluded that strong evidence exists for correlations between facial activity and degree of subjective emotion and, furthermore, that "the experimental evidence suggest that facial efference may play an important causal role in the subjective experience of emotion" (p. 273).

Further evidence has suggested that artificial manipulation of the facial muscles could influence affective responses to standard stimuli (Duclos, Laird, Schneider, Sexter, Stern, & Van Lighten, 1989; Laird, 1974) and recall of affect-laden material (Laird, Wagener, Halal, & Szegda, 1982), even when the subject is unaware of the purpose behind the manipulation. Posed facial expression are not identical with naturally occurring expressions (Hess & Kleck, 1990), and the evidence with posed facial expressions is weaker than that with naturally occurring expressions (Ekman, 1993). However, it does seem to be consistent with the facial feedback hypothesis (Adelman & Zajonc, 1989).

Manipulation of posture has also been shown to influence affective reactions (Duclos et al., 1989; Riskind, 1984). Similarly, manipulation of gesture may affect emotion. Tom, Petterson, Lau, Burton, and Cook (1991) asked subjects to nod or shake their heads while listening to material through headphones, under the pretext that this was to test the quality of sound production. These movements affected preferences. More recently,

Cacioppo, Priester, and Berntson (1993) produced data that suggest that arm flexion during exposure to neutral stimuli is associated with positive evaluations of those stimuli. Cacioppo et al. (1993) argued that flexing the arm is intrinsically related to the acquisition of desired objects. Therefore, it might automatically produce a positive emotional tone that would then come to be associated with the neutral stimulus. Hypotheses such as this, although clearly in need of further evaluation, suggest that many noncognitive factors may be involved in emotional reactions.

Such findings have implications for the objective measurement of emotions and the possibility of direct manipulation as a component of therapeutic interventions. This is an area in its infancy with enormous difficulties in measurement and in inference, but these results, taken together, indicate that it is possible to obtain reliable measures of emotion that do not depend on self-reports of hypothetical cognitive variables.

Further evidence that the relation between facial expression and subjective experience may be reciprocal has come from investigations (Kleck et al., 1976; Lanzetta, Cartwright-Smith, & Kleck, 1976) of the effects of being observed on subjects' reactions to electric shock. Subjects who knew they were being observed produced significantly fewer expressive reactions to the shocks, and this in turn was associated with lower autonomic and subjective responses.

Cacioppo, Petty, and Tassinary (1989), reviewing the field of social psychophysiology, argued that although physiology and emotion are not identical, it might be possible to draw strong inferences about a person's subjective experience on the basis of physiological measures. Although "attitudes and emotions have traditionally been defined, at least within social psychology, in terms of what people report believing or feeling" (Cacioppo et al., 1989, p. 78), psychophysiology might provide a clearer understanding of the processes involved in these apparently purely subjective phenomena.

Evidence of physiological involvement during therapy with clinical populations is limited, and what little there is appears contradictory. For example, Baker, Cannon, Tiffany, and Gino (1984) measured the amplitude of the heart rate response during aversion therapy and found it to predict maintenance of behavior change. The greater the heart rate response, the better the maintenance of appropriate behavior.

However, Leitenberg, Agras, Butz, and Wincze (1971), with nine phobics undergoing systematic desensitization, found a variety of relations between heart rate and behavior change. Vermilyea, Boice, and Barlow (1984) observed desynchrony between behavioral and physiological indices to occur during therapy for agoraphobia, but level of synchrony at termination of therapy was not predictive of success with behavior change. However, Michelson and Mavissakalian (1985), testing a similar client population, found synchronizers to show better outcomes than nonsynchronizers.

Psychophysiological measures have been used with increasing frequency in the developing field of social psychophysiology (e.g., Cacioppo & Petty, 1983; Wagner & Manstead, 1989). Cacioppo and Petty (1981) reviewed evidence for physiological involvement in word recognition tasks and in attitude development and change, concluding that increased muscle activity in the body parts is associated with speech during these cognitive activities. Cacioppo, Petty, and Morris (1985) found the degree and type of muscle activity to be associated with the cognitive effort required. Social facilitation effects also appeared to be associated with physiological reactions (Moore & Baron, 1983).

The recent work in social and behavioral psychophysiology provides a stronger empirical basis for some theoretical models of affect. The field has, of course, a very long way to go. However, the investigation of physiological concomitants of emotional distress and of the physical effects of behavior therapy may be valuable in the development of a clearer understanding of affect that is not limited by the assumption that conscious thought is the only variable of interest.

CONCLUSION

The assumption that cognition is always prior to emotion is open to empirical challenge. Cognitive–behavioral research has tended to theory-confirming rather than theory-testing designs (Greenwald et al., 1986). Research that purports to study influences on human behavior frequently fails to measure any behavior other than questionnaire completion. Because of the assumption that anything that isn't cognition isn't psychology, there is a tendency toward premature closure before environmental, biological, and physiological variables have been adequately explored.

It is clear that models of human behavior based on the completion of questionnaires are less than ideal. However, the assumption that cognition is the only relevant cause of human behavior is so strong that psychologists seem more likely to continue to elaborate cognitively based theories than they are to seek alternatives. In the following chapter, I explore recent developments of a concept that goes back to Freud and beyond—the concept of unconscious, but definitely cognitive, influences on cognition.

Chapter 5

Unconscious Cognition: Elaboration of Ideas to Shore Up a Failing Paradigm

> *Most, if not all, of our currently held ideas and theories about mental processes are wrong.*
>
> —Tulving (1985, p. 386)

The earlier chapters of this book have illustrated some of the problems that arise from an assumption that all human behavior is the result of conscious or at least reportable thought. In this chapter, I examine the concept of *unconscious cognition*, a concept that has been argued to provide a solution to these problems. But this, too, provides only an illusion of explanation.

The evidence that conscious thought does not control all human action is incontrovertible (e.g., Jacoby, Toth, Lindsay, & Debner, 1992). As Bruner (1992) pointed out, most skilled behaviors, as well as most frequently performed behaviors, are carried out with little or no conscious awareness, and the performers are frequently at a loss to explain precisely what they are doing or how they are doing it.

The unconscious cognition response to this evidence, however, has been guided by another untested, largely unacknowledged, assumption that cognition of some sort is the only cause of behavior that a psychologist may legitimately hypothesize. This, in turn, is based on a fundamental epistemological assumption that an exclusive focus on thought is the only appropriate strategy for understanding how individual human beings operate (Schnaitter, 1987b). This assumption leads theorists not to the search for alternative, noncognitive views of human behavior, but rather to the seemingly inevitable proposal that another type of cognition must exist and that this must provide the missing explanatory variables.

UNCONSCIOUS COGNITION
AS THE ONLY ALTERNATIVE

Brewin (1989) conceded that "there is ample evidence that conscious thought is not a necessary determinant of behavior" (p. 384), but assumed that any behavior not determined by immediate conscious thought was necessarily "attributable to non-conscious cognitive processes" (p. 381). The concept that there are no cognitive processes involved, that it is not necessary to invoke cognition in order to explain human behavior, is not a legitimate consideration within this particular view.

In a similar vein, Kruglanski and Klar (1985) asked, "Do people know what they are doing? ... Are human actions thoughtful and rational or are they often mindless and automatic?" (p. 41). Their view of the possible range of alternative explanations was limited by the assumption that some sort of cognition must be the root cause of all human behavior. By asking, "Are they [i.e. human actions] consciously determined or do they frequently stem from unconscious forces inaccessible to human cognizance?" (p. 41), Kruglanski and Klar (1985) implied that only two alternatives were possible. If an action is not controlled by conscious thought, then, by definition, it must be controlled by unconscious thought. Furthermore, unconscious thoughts must be inaccessible, and therefore human behavior must remain mysterious and can never be understood scientifically.

Jacoby et al. (1992) argued that "it is clear that people sometimes plan and then act. More often than not, however, behavior is influenced by unconscious processes; that is, we act and then, if questioned, make our excuses" (p. 82). Again, the assumption is that, if someone acts without any conscious planning, that person must have been "influenced by unconscious processes." Is it not possible that, sometimes, people simply *act*? At least some of the time, at least some behaviors may well be straightforward (although by no means simple) responses to environmental stimuli. Habitual behavior, for example, may involve little or no cognitive activity and therefore is unlikely to be explained by any model that depends on cognitions (Kristiansen, 1987).

The invocation of unconscious processes, without definition or refinement, adds nothing of any utility to an explanation of behavior. However, it appears that, within the contemporary psychological literature, reference to processes of some kind or cognitions of some kind must be made in order to legitimize statements about human action. The concept that, in at least some situations, some actions are simply performed, without the accompaniment or antecedent of anything that can meaningfully be called cognition at all, is completely outside the frame of reference of most contemporary theories.

It is interesting to note, parenthetically, that no such limitation seems to arise in explaining animal behavior. Hickey (1994) argued that one reason why behaviorists encounter considerable hostility from the mainstream is that a behavioral view runs counter to the predominant philosophy that human behavior is different from that of other animals; it is the result of mysterious factors lying outside the natural world and inaccessible to scientific investigation. Thus, behaviorism conflicts with comfortable views of the human being as special and different.

When animals are shown to act in ways that can be attributable in humans to thought processes (e.g., Epstein, Kirshnit, Lanza, & Rubin, 1984), the theoretical alternatives that are proposed are somewhat different from those arising in the case of human behavior. Arguments revolve not around the alternative explanations of conscious thought and unconscious thought, but around the alternatives of conscious thought or no thought at all (Robertson, 1987). Other animals, it appears, can act without cognition, but for some reason human beings can not.

Massey (1993) challenged psychologists to be more explicit about whether their models apply to humans only or to animals in general and argued that a psychological model that does not hold for nonhuman animals, unless there is compelling evidence why it should not, is an incomplete and unsatisfactory one. Wasserman (1993), too, has argued that we must assume an underlying continuity between the processes underlying human behavior and those underlying similar behavior in other animals. He reviewed evidence that demonstrated complex memory and the component skills underlying numeracy and language in other animals and suggested that, if it were possible to study these attributes without reference to cognitive models, then it should be possible to do the same with related human attributes.

UNCONSCIOUS COGNITION AS AN ESCAPE CLAUSE IN PSYCHOLOGICAL THEORIES

Without an objective definition of nonconscious thought processes, the proposition that they cause behavior is unfalsifiable. The concept of unconscious cognition may be seen as an example of a general tendency to continue to elaborate an existing paradigm and to accept arguments of a less stringent nature in order to maintain a belief in the legitimacy of a particular world view (Lakatos, 1978). If one is unwilling to challenge the assumption that cognition causes all human behavior, one then must assume that a behavior that is not related to any conscious cognition must, ipso facto, be caused by some new, imaginary type of cognition that nobody can see.

Researchers in the fields of memory and perception in particular have made extensive use of the notion of unconscious cognition. The concept is applied to the explanation of behaviors that have been learned, but the behaver has no clear idea of how the learning was done. Concepts falling into this category include procedural knowledge, implicit memory, knowledge without awareness, and a range of similar hypothetical entities. People clearly acquire many skills without necessarily remembering how they acquired them and respond to many perceptual stimuli without noticing that they are doing so.

One strand of evidence comes from research with individuals with specific neurological deficits. Clinical research has indicated that amnesics and prosopagnosics respond differently to previously encountered events and faces than to novel stimuli (Kihlstrom, Barnardt, & Tataryn, 1992a), even though they have no conscious recollection of them. Weiskrantz (1986), among others, demonstrated that people who have lost all awareness of visual stimuli as a result of brain surgery are still able to respond accurately to objects in their field of vision. Related abilities have been identified in patients suffering from deafness or anaesthesia: They are able to respond to familiar stimuli although they show no awareness of them (Kihlstrom et al., 1992b).

The unspoken assumption behind much of this research is that behavior occurring without conscious awareness is anomalous and restricted to those with neurological abnormalities (Cacioppo et al., 1989). Research with normal samples, however, has shown similar, although less dramatic, results: People frequently act on the basis of stimuli and previous events of which they have no conscious awareness (for a recent collection of contemporary explanations, see Bornstein & Pittman, 1992). The underlying, seemingly unchallengeable assumption behind contemporary interpretations of such evidence is that some cognitive process must be involved in all human memory and all interpretation of perceptual stimuli. If the behaver cannot describe a cognitive process, then one must be occurring at an unconscious level.

Writing specifically about this issue in memory research, Hirst and Gazzaniga (1988) expressed doubt about the utility proposing two separate cognitive systems, one conscious and one unconscious. They pointed out that, in contemporary memory research, "one of the more interesting distinctions in the literature and one of the most poorly understood is the one that variously goes under the labels 'procedural' versus 'declarative' memories, 'explicit' versus 'implicit' memories, 'semantic' versus 'episodic' memories, and memory 'with awareness' or 'without awareness'" (pp. 296–297). On the basis of an exhaustive literature review, Hirst and Gazzaniga (1988) concluded that "the distinction between procedural and declarative memory (and related distinctions) still needs a strong theoretical foundation if it is to prove useful" (p. 305).

Thus, Hirst and Gazzaniga argued that "research that would aggressively determine the empirical basis for such distinctions as procedural versus declarative memory should be encouraged" (p. 298). Hypothesizing two different kinds of memory was of no help at all, either in developing a general understanding of memory or in dealing with specific individuals with memory problems, unless it was supported by rigorous scientific models that could predict how the two types of memory worked.

The contention that the concept of unconscious cognition is a vague one that has been insufficiently elaborated to have any place in scientific models of human behavior is strengthened when one examines the conflicting claims made about unconscious cognition. On the one hand, a group of theorists (e.g., Lewicki, Hill, & Czyzewska, 1992) argue that unconscious cognition is sophisticated, complex, and rapid—generally a form of information processing superior to conscious thought. On the other hand, other theorists (e.g., Greenwald, 1992) claim that unconscious cognition is restricted to fairly simple feats of memory, recognition, and the straightforward processing of perceptual input. As Locke (1994) argued in a recent account of contemporary control theory, a theory that explains human behavior in computer–metaphor terms, "control theory ... appears to be whatever the most recent control theorists says it is" (p. 368). These issues are of crucial importance in basic cognitive science, but they become even more central when one moves away from the laboratory and examines the application of these and related concepts in therapeutic contexts.

UNCONSCIOUS COGNITION AS AN ESCAPE CLAUSE IN COGNITIVE THERAPY

Applied research and model building in cognitive therapy has, in the past decades, tended to adopt the concept of nonconscious cognition and also to avoid consideration of the possibility that noncognitive explanations may, at least some of the time, be more parsimonious and more useful. A basic criterion of science is that unobservables must be related to observable phenomena from which they can be inferred. The assessment of unconscious perception and unconscious cognition in laboratory-based cognitive research has been the subject of rigorous debate. However, Merikle and Reingold (1992) recently concluded that there is still no universally satisfactory method for the measurement of these and related concepts.

The problems of measurement of concepts and of their relations to observable events become even more difficult when dealing with clinical populations and when attempting to conduct research in more ecologically valid, clinically relevant contexts.

Hard data exist indicating the presence of subtle, unintentional, behavioral differences between people with and without emotional problems. Research using Stroop tasks has demonstrated that emotionally distressed individuals may show differences in color-naming latencies for different classes of word (see MacLeod, 1991, for a review). Much of this work has been characterized by strong, direct links between hypothesized unconscious cognitive processes and clearly defined behaviors or physiological events. In these instances, the premise that these unconscious cognitions exist leads to specific, testable hypotheses.

Although the Stroop research itself (e.g., Hope, Rapee, Heimberg, & Dombeck, 1990; Mathews & MacLeod, 1985) has frequently been rigorously designed and conducted, at least some researchers have generalized well beyond the limits of their data. For example, Hope et al. (1990) interpreted the findings of their Stroop studies as providing empirical support for Beck's (1993) concept of self-schemata. Hope et al. (1990) found that social phobics took significantly longer to name the colors of words associated with negative emotions than they did to name the colors of neutral words; this, they concluded, provided support for a hypersensitivity to negative social evaluation among these subjects, as hypothesized by Beck. Such an interpretation, however intuitively appealing, is not science but a leap of faith, prompted by an unexamined assumption that unconscious cognitions exist and that they somehow play an important role in determining response latencies.

The relation between a hypothetical and unconscious sensitivity to negative evaluation and a relative delay in the color-naming of words like *shameful* or *embarrassed* (Hope et al., 1990) is a loose and nonscientific one. Nor is the existence, or direction, of this relationship specifically hypothesized by Beck's theory. Had these researchers found no relation, they could have argued that result to be consistent with Beck's theories, in that the Stroop task does not involve normal social interaction and as such may not activate the hypothetical self-schema that includes sensitivity to negative social evaluation.

Alternatively, a decrease in latencies among socially phobic individuals to emotionally laden target words could also be argued to support Beck's model. One could argue, for example, that these words were congruent with an existing cognitive schema among the socially phobic individuals and therefore should not require as much attention as neutral control words. Accordingly, nondisturbed individuals, who are presumably not primed with a sensitivity to these words, should respond more slowly.

It is clear that a theory that can be adduced to support all these mutually contradictory hypotheses is a theory that actually supports none of them. Furthermore, problems of interpretation such as this are not a function of poor experimental control or inappropriate data collection. It is not the design of the research studies that is at fault; it is the theoretical model itself. Collection of empirical data will not prove or disprove models that invoke vague and nonobservable processes such as self-schemata and associative networks because they are not grounded in empirical observation.

Other research has failed to support the findings of Hope et al. (1990), let alone distinguish among explanatory models. Another Stroop study (Mathews & Klug, 1993) showed that clinically anxious subjects responded more slowly than controls, not only to words related to social anxiety (e.g., *shaking, crazy*) but also to words related to a lack of anxiety (e.g., *fearless, safe*). Mathews and Klug (1993) argued that this finding could be explained by the semantic associations between the positive words and the specific emotional concerns of the patient. Thus, they argued, positive words activated hypothetical associative networks and evoked their antonyms, which in turn activated the hypothetical self-schema. Nonrelated but positive control words did not.

By contrast, Lavy, van Oppen, and van den Hout (1994) conducted an almost identical study to that of Mathews and Klug (1993), with obsessive–compulsive subjects rather than clinically anxious ones. They found interference in the Stroop test only with negative obsession-related words (e.g., *guilt, fail*) and not with positive obsession-related words (e.g., *safe, protected*).

To confuse the issue further, Rapee, McCallum, Melville, Ravenscroft, and Rodney (1994) used a recall-based technique to examine semantic biases in social phobics. In four studies, they failed to find evidence for a bias toward any particular class of word, again failing to support cognitive, semantic network explanations of anxiety-related symptoms. Although there are major unresolved issues in methodology in this research area, these ambiguities and contradictions can only be identified because the research has been rigorously conducted and rigorously described and because some objective data were included in the designs of these projects.

Many other theories in contemporary clinical psychology postulate unconscious cognitions that are not related at all, not even in the indirect and ambiguous way in which Hope et al. (1990) and Mathews and Klug (1993) related self-schemata to response latencies, to observable events. In such instances, unconscious cognition becomes an escape clause. Rather than explaining behavior, it serves to explain away any inconvenient facts that fail to accord with the predictions of cognitive theories. If cognition, as assessed by self-report, is not an accurate predictor of behavior, then the only solution seems to be to invent another sort of cognition, one that nobody can see, and claim that it provides the explanation. Propositions of this kind illustrate the problems inherent in being unable or unwilling to challenge a particular paradigm.

Guidano and Liotti (1983), for example, proposed a model of emotional problems based on hypothetical variables that are unobservable, not only in practice but in principle. The theory holds that these unobservables cannot be observed or reported by the individual who is hypothesized to be experiencing them, nor can they be inferred by reference to any other variable. The hypothesized causal chains are described in so loose a manner that it is impossible to specify any observable behavior or self-report that can be unambiguously argued to result from any of the unobservable variables.

Models such as this possess all the problems outlined in chapter 2 with reference to self-efficacy theory, with the additional problem that the crucial variables are not susceptible to any form of assessment, not even self-reports, which, with all their acknowledged problems, may still be regarded as having some indicative value.

The more general concept of unconscious cognition has been used to elaborate cognitive theories of behavior for centuries. Freud used it (Freud, 1910/1962), and it continues to exist in modern cognitive theory (e.g., Guidano & Liotti, 1983). Epstein (1994) argued that the persistence of the concept, despite good scientific reasons for rejecting it, is an indication of its appeal to our sense of ourselves as complex beings with attributes that go beyond the merely physical. To reiterate, unconscious cognitions are hypothetical entities, thoughts that influence behavior but are unobservable, not only directly but indirectly through their effects, and not only by the world at large, but also by the person within whose mind they are hypothesized to be taking place (Greenwald, 1992).

There are two general views on nonconscious cognitions. One is that the thinker is never aware of them and can never become aware of them (e.g., Greenwald, 1992; Guidano & Liotti, 1983). The other is that one is not aware of them at the time they influence behavior but might become aware of them later (e.g., Freud, 1910/1962).

The first view can easily be rejected. A nonphysical event that is completely unobservable, not merely in practice but in principle as well, and that has no clearly identified relation to any observable event, has no place in science. Any theory that relies on such imaginary phenomena can most usefully be rejected.

For the second alternative, the view that something called cognition, completely outside conscious awareness, may occur and influence behavior with awareness coming later, there is a more parsimonious explanation. The cognition may better be understood as a post hoc explanation of behavior (Warshaw & Davis, 1985), produced specifically in response to a question from an experimenter or therapist. As there is not, and by definition cannot be, any direct evidence that the cognition had any existence before it was "recalled" by the subject, calling it an unconscious cognition only confuses the issue.

Despite the fact that it was precisely a rejection of introspection that led to the development of modern scientific psychology, many contemporary psychologists seem to regard introspective reflection as error free, a useful source of data in the experimental context and a healthy and desirable activity in the clinical context (Wilson, Dunn, Kraft, & Lisle, 1989). Wilson et al. (1989), however, argued that introspection is subject to demand characteristics. They presented evidence that, when asked to introspect, people (whether experimental subjects or clients in therapy) experienced strong social pressure to come up with a good story, one that conformed to lay theories about human motivations. Specifically, Wilson et al. (1989) proposed the existence of a learned, socially reinforced tendency to explain one's own behavior by reference to personal attitudes to the object or event under consideration rather than to the social context or expectancies. They also proposed that people attempt to find a reason for the particular attitude or idea; social expectations demand that individuals have reasons for their actions, for it is socially unacceptable, when asked to explain an action or expressed attitude, to say "I don't know why I did that or believe that."

In an empirical study, Wilson, Hodges, and LaFleur (1995) demonstrated that it was possible to manipulate the reasons that people give for their behavior by manipulating their recall of aspects of the target situation. Thus, recalled reasons for behavior may be better understood as constructions, produced after the fact in response to an experimenter's question. Moreover, research in which people received posthypnotic instructions to perform a particular action and were then asked to explain that action, for example, has demonstrated a strong tendency for people to produce internal, cognitive, explanations for their own behaviors, even when those behaviors appear to others to be caused by public, external factors (Hilgard, 1986).

Thus, respondents create thoughts to fit their behaviors. Wilson et al. (1989) argued further that this process would lead to an artificial attitude or opinion heavily based on specific cognitions. This, in turn, may be quite unlike the process by which people spontaneously understand their behaviors or form opinions about events and may well be an inappropriate strategy for regulating behavior. Illustrating this point, Wilson and LaFleur (1995) showed that asking participants to analyze their reasons for behaving in a certain way in a hypothetical situation had the effect of changing their predictions but not their behavior itself. As Wilson et al. (1989) put it, "under some circumstances, people are better off not thinking about why they feel the way they do" (p. 289).

USING UNCONSCIOUS COGNITION TO BOLSTER THE POSTCOGNITIVE VIEW OF EMOTION

The concept of unconscious cognition is used not only as a strategy for explaining behavior when conscious cognitions fail to do so but also as a strategy for explaining emotional states. Zajonc and colleagues (e.g., Zajonc, 1984; Zajonc & Markus, 1984, 1985; Zajonc et al., 1989), as discussed in chapter 4, have argued against the widespread view that emotion arises subsequent to and as a result of cognitive appraisal. One response to these arguments (Parrott & Sabini, 1989) provides an interesting example of the invocation of unconscious cognition to deny the validity of alternatives to mainstream views, in this case to the mainstream conception of human emotion.

Zajonc (1984), in a highly controversial paper, argued that affect, unlike cognition, was effortless, immediate, automatic, uncontrollable, and irrevocable by deliberate thought. These characteristics suggested that it was not postcognitive in nature. Parrot and Sabini (1989) responded by inventing a type of unconscious, automatic cognition that had all these properties and claiming that it was prior to emotion. Because the new type of cognition is unconscious, experimental subjects are unable to report on it and thus it is necessary to take its existence on faith. This notion, they claimed, provided a "secure theoretical basis" (p. 49) for the primacy of cognition.

Parrott and Sabini (1989), like many other writers in this area, appeared to be allowing themselves to be constrained by the unacknowledged assumptions not just of modern psychology, but more broadly of contemporary epistemology as well (Schnaitter, 1987b). They started from the observation that behaviors and emotions often seem to be caused by stimuli of which the individual is not aware, a proposition with which few people of any theoretical orientation would disagree. They then went on to assume that these stimuli must be cognitions, because cognitions cause everything. By arbitrarily defining all nonconscious influences on behavior as cognitions, they appear to have won the argument by default. In fact, they have simply produced a circular, nonverifiable, nonscientific justification for their own point of view. It is clear that variables that are by definition unobservable to anyone cannot play a part in scientific explanations, unless these unobservable variables are clearly and unambiguously related to other observable variables.

Brewin (1989) used a related argument to tackle a more general issue. He dealt with some problems in cognitive theories by arguing for two cognitive systems, one conscious and one nonconscious. The conscious system (defined as knowledge that is verbally accessible), he argued, could be influenced in unspecified ways by the nonconscious system, producing behavior that appeared to be at odds with self-reported intentions or beliefs. Such a model, being in principle unfalsifiable, adds nothing to the explanation of human behavior. It simply provides an escape clause.

CONCLUSION

It may be seen as overly cynical to contend that theoretical elaborations of the type described in this chapter look like attempts to shore up a paradigm that simply does not work. However, sociological theorists have argued that the invocation of invisible and ineffable forces for the specific purpose of explaining away any deviations between prediction and actuality is a characteristic of closed belief systems (see Goffman, 1961).

The primacy-of-cognition paradigm, the notion that cognition is central, primary, and essential to all human behavior, may be an example of a closed belief system. If one is convinced that cognition is central to behavior, and if one's models fail to support this conviction, it may be natural to elaborate the existing model by inventing another sort of cognition and tacking it on, rather than rejecting the model and seeking radically different alternatives, even though the elaboration occurs at the expense of the scientific integrity of the resulting model.

The assumption that all human behavior is controlled by cognition has its roots in the history of ideas; Descartes' famous statement "I think therefore I am" encapsulated a deeply felt conviction that runs throughout Western civilization. In the next chapter, I deal in more detail with the possibility that at least some human behavior, including some highly skilled and complex activities, occurs without the involvement of anything that can meaningfully be called cognition.

Chapter 6

Unseating Cognition: Behavior Independent of Conscious Thought

There would seem to be little doubt that a considerable amount of human behavior occurs without awareness of the behavior at the time of its occurrence.

—Eriksen (1960, p. 297)

In the previous chapters, I presented evidence and arguments that cause difficulties for a model that regards cognition as the prime cause of all human behavior. Chapters 4 and 5 demonstrated that the invocation of cognitive determinants cannot provide a complete explanation for many aspects of human behavior and emotion and outlined arguments for the rejection of cognition-centered views of human behavior. This chapter continues the argument for the possibility that at least some human behavior occurs in the absence of anything that can meaningfully be referred to as cognition.

Schnaitter (1987b) argued that "if there is a common thread to modern philosophical orthodoxy it is that the problem of knowledge will be resolved in thinking about thought. But if there is one bit of advice in the work of B. F. Skinner, one insight which runs contrary to the mainstream, it is that something is badly muddled in this whole history of thought about thought" (p. 57). At least some aspects of human behavior may be best explained by viewing cognition as a result of behavior. The underlying assumption of such a model is not that we behave in the way we do because of the way we think but that we think the way we do because of the way we see ourselves behave.

The idea that cognitions arise as a direct result of our observation of our own behavior has a long history in social psychology. One of the areas of research supporting this notion most strongly is the theory of cognitive dissonance (e.g., Festinger, 1957). It has been established over decades of research that people who are persuaded to act in ways that contradict their previously stated beliefs will tend to alter their subsequent cognitions in a way that makes them more consistent with their observed behavior.

The phenomenon is far more complex than this, but it does support a postbehavioral view of cognition. Self-perception theories (e.g., Bem, 1972; Nisbett & Valins, 1971) have also provided extensive evidence that individuals do not have privileged access to internal information about themselves. Rather, actors use the same principles as other people in predicting their own future behavior and inferring from their previous behavior. Thus, reports of cognitive variables such as attributions and attitudes may be seen as post hoc explanations of what one has seen oneself do, not as the causes of those actions (Wilson, 1985).

DEVELOPMENT OF PREFERENCES WITHOUT COGNITIVE INVOLVEMENT

The mere exposure effect, the finding that exposure to a stimulus increases liking for that stimulus without any conscious mediation, was first demonstrated by Kunst-Wilson and Zajonc (1980). They showed that affective reactions to neutral stimuli become more positive with repeated exposure to those stimuli and that this effect is independent of any conscious awareness of having seen the stimuli before. They found that research subjects expressed greater liking for shapes that had been shown to them previously than for new shapes. Most importantly, subjects were unable to state with any degree of accuracy whether they had seen the shapes before, suggesting that exposure had an effect on preference without any conscious awareness of familiarity.

Since this original study, over 200 published papers have replicated and extended these findings (Bornstein, 1992). Interestingly, Bornstein concluded that the more accurate subjects were in recognizing the stimuli to which they had previously been exposed, the smaller was the effect on their preferences, suggesting that the mere exposure effect of preference for the familiar may positively depend on a lack of conscious awareness.

Such phenomena have been explained in the terms that were rejected in the previous chapter, that is, by recourse to unconscious cognition. Tsal (1985), for example, asserted that the evidence on liking without recognition must be explicable by unconscious cognition. In response, Zajonc and Markus (1985) pointed out that this view "rests on the assumption that in those affective experiences where an antecedent cognitive process cannot be directly demonstrated, an unconscious cognitive process must have taken place ... unless Tsal can show just how—and in what form—an unconscious cognitive antecedent was involved in a given affective reaction, his proposition is unfalsifiable" (p. 363).

The cognition-centered models seem to regard introspection as incontrovertibly accurate. What we report is assumed to be what we think. However, as discussed earlier, Wilson, Dunn, Kraft, and Lisle (1989) argued that the act of explaining our actions or emotions is an unnatural one which may have a disruptive effect; thus, research relying on self-reports of decision processes must suffer from biases. Wilson et al. (1989) argued that when people are invited to introspect, particularly in the context of an experiment, they feel compelled to come up with a reasonable-sounding account and to focus on attitudes and thought processes that appear to be logical and relevant to the issue.

Tryon (1982) proposed that consistency between verbal reports and behavior was a culturally determined, learned characteristic. This view is supported by cross-cultural work (Rogoff & Chavajay, 1995). Kashima, Siegal, Tanaka, and Kashima (1992) found differences between Japanese and Australian students in the extent to which they expected attitude and behavior to be consistent. In Japanese society, it may be natural to display some inconsistency; indeed, in many cultures, the acceptance of ambiguity and inconsistency in behavior and opinion is regarded as a positive aspect of mature wisdom (Markus & Kitayama, 1991). It may well be that it is natural for people to display inconsistency and not to have sound reasons for their behavior until they are asked to think of some.

Research examining voting behavior among American adults (Granberg & Brown, 1989) demonstrated that affect was important in deciding which way to vote but reportable cognitions were rather less so. One third of respondents expressed clear views on the relative desirability of different political parties despite the fact that they "cannot (or at least do not) tell us why they feel as they do" (p. 172). As the authors pointed out, "it may be a slight exaggeration to say that people who give no reasons ... have no cognitions" (p. 179), but "many of the respondents did not have relevant, salient thoughts ready" (pp. 179–180). This suggests that political preferences, at least in some cases, are not derived from a rational consideration of the facts but depend on other, noncognitive factors. If this is the case for political preferences, it may well be the case for other choices that we have been taught to assume will have a sound, rational, cognitive basis. Granberg and Brown (1989) suggested that if the participants in their survey "had been given the questions a week in advance, they might have thought of reasons" (p. 179), but their conclusion was that, in the case of choosing how to vote, a responsible decision made by competent adults, cognition seemed to play no role at all for a large number of people.

In a similar vein, Slovic (1995) reviewed evidence that demonstrated that different questions could elicit different preferences in the same circumstances. Rather than a set of ready-made preferences somewhere inside people's heads, "preferences are ... constructed on the spot by an adaptive decision maker" (p. 369).

In the remaining sections of this chapter I argue that many cases of human behavior may occur without anything that may meaningfully be called cognition being involved at all, except perhaps if people are asked to explain their actions afterwards.

ACTION WITHOUT CONSCIOUS THOUGHT

Habit Versus Unconscious Control

It is easy to demonstrate the existence of instances in which cognition does not direct behavior. Research on action slips (e.g., Norman, 1981; Sellen, 1994) and absent-mindedness (e.g., Reason, 1977, 1979, 1984; Reason & Lucas, 1984) has classified everyday occurrences in which individuals have behaved in ways other than intended. Familiar examples include situations in which a person intends to do one thing but does another, such as putting salt instead of sugar into coffee; in which a person starts to carry out an intention but does not complete it, such as leaving one's office to get an envelope and coming back without it; and in which a person confuses two intentions, such as answering the telephone with "Come in." Self-report studies focusing on driving have suggested that slips of this nature are not intentional and are quite different from the deliberate violation of rules (Reason, Manstead, Stradling, Baxter, & Campbell, 1990).

Related research (e.g., Reason, 1984; Sellen, 1994) has used diary techniques to elicit self-reports of action slips. This research showed that slips occurred mainly when the intended action was common and frequent. A similar frequent action would be substituted for or otherwise interfere with the intended one. For example, a person might intend to put a carton of milk in the refrigerator but instead put it in the dishwasher. Interestingly, Reason's (1984) survey found that such slips were most likely to happen in familiar and relaxed circumstances and not under conditions of stress or uncertainty.

It might be argued that research of this type illustrates that things can go wrong when we're not thinking and thus merely proves the point that thinking is important. However, an alternative argument is that behaving independent of cognitive processes is the norm, that we do it all the time, and that we only become aware that we are doing so when things go wrong. These trivial events may involve the same processes that are involved in catastrophic human error accidents in industry (Reason, 1990a; Wagenaar, Hudson, & Reason, 1990), and literature on ergonomic design, based on the assumption that people frequently act other than as planned (e.g., Dörner & Schaub, 1994; Reason, 1990b; Wagenaar & Reason, 1990; Zapf & Reason, 1994), is growing.

Besides the practical implications, instances of actions other than those intended raise interesting questions from the perspective of social cognitive models of behavior. Why, given an (apparent) intention to perform the correct behavior, the physical skills, and the opportunity to perform the behavior, does the behavior not occur? As Mixon (1991) argued, contemporary cognitive theories are unable to explain situations in which a person intends to perform a particular action but does not.

Warshaw and Davis (1985) argued that intentions need to be distiguished from expectations of one's behavior. Expectations based on previous behaviors are better predictors of behavior than are intentions for a number of reasons. First, many habitual behaviors do not involve decisions (i.e., no cognitive process is involved in choosing this behavior rather than another), and thus intention is irrelevant; the behavior simply happens. Second, many behaviors are defined in terms of goals rather than actions, which means one cannot be sure that one will achieve what one intends or expects. Third, intentions may change in ways that expectations may not. Expectations, according to Warshaw and Davis (1985), are not determinants of behavior at all, but reflections of what one knows of one's typical previous behavior.

It is clear that many tasks that are carried out frequently, both simple and complex actions, are done without conscious involvement. For example, complex tasks done routinely, such as driving home from work, are normally carried out with no conscious awareness at all. The driver typically only becomes aware of not being consciously in control of his or her behavior in unusual circumstances, such as "waking up" to discover that he or she has arrived at home when the actual intention was to go somewhere else. Bruner (1992), in a discussion of the unconscious, noted that most highly skilled behavior is performed without conscious involvement, and indeed people who can perform complex skills are often at a loss to describe how they do it.

However, Bruner's explanation of this was, again, the one most commonly raised to explain automatic behaviors. That is, that if actions are not controlled by conscious cognition, then they must be controlled by some unobservable unconscious cognition, a conclusion already rejected as unscientific and unfalsifiable. This chapter presents an alternative view, that nothing that can usefully be referred to as cognition is involved at all.

The driving example, along with typing, playing a musical instrument, and so forth, may be seen as examples of repetitive, overlearned skills and thus as a category of special cases—overlearned everyday activities that occur without conscious control. However, there is increasing evidence to suggest that the complex and dynamic behaviors involved in social interactions may also best be explained without recourse to cognition.

Complex Spontaneous Behaviors: Noncognitive or Unconscious Cognition?

The ability to coordinate verbal exchanges and nonverbal behavior during conversation is a complex activity (e.g., Hadar, Steiner, & Rose, 1985) that occurs without conscious effort or control (Hatfield, Cacioppo, & Rapson, 1992). In fact, it has been argued (e.g., Davis, 1985) that coordinated social behavior of this nature can only be done naturally and that conscious efforts to produce it will not normally succeed unless carried out by highly trained actors. In particular, it appears that the orderly conduct of social interactions, including not only the mechanics of turn taking in speech and movement but also the ability to get on well or establish rapport, is controlled by patterns of behavior of which both the behaver and the observer are completely unaware (Bernieri & Rosenthal, 1991).

This phenomenon has been observed both during relatively circumscribed social interactions and in overall, longer term patterns of interaction. Hayes and Cobb (1982), for example, observed the routines of two people who lived together in artificial isolation for a month. Conversation was found to occur in regular cycles of approximately 90 minutes. These cycles were so regular and so entirely outside the awareness of the subjects, that Hayes and Cobb (1982) concluded that conversational behavior must, in part, be affected by factors other than a conscious wish to communicate.

The quality, as well as the frequency, of social interaction seems to be affected by noncognitive factors. The ability to react appropriately to emotional responses in others, for example, is a highly complex social activity that appears to occur without the need for conscious thought (Öhman, 1988). Vocal characteristics such as loudness and pitch clearly play a role in conveying emotion (Kappas, Hess, & Scherer, 1991), but only the skilled and practiced actor can produce these vocal characteristics at will.

The phenomenon of rapport, of getting on well with someone, has been the subject of some recent research focused on specific, short-term social interactions. The experience of rapport appears to be a pleasurable one (Tickle-Degnen & Rosenthal, 1987) that cannot be attained through conscious effort, in part because it appears to arise from the interaction rather than from any action of a single individual. Nonverbal behavior in particular appears to be important in determining level of rapport.

Rime and Schiaratura (1991), reviewing the role of gesture in communication, noted that people normally engaged in nonverbal behaviors directly related to their own speech patterns, particularly when discussing personally involving material. However, the function of these nonverbal behaviors did not appear to be involved with the conscious communication of information. Speakers were found to engage in the same behaviors with equal frequency, regardless of whether the other member of the dyad could see them or not, for example when conversing by telephone.

Furthermore, related research on gesture (Rime & Schiaratura, 1991) showed that inability to see the gestures (for example, by listening to taped conversation) did not lead to any loss of communication, whereas presentation of the nonverbal gestures without speech (e.g., by watching a video without the soundtrack) did not allow the receiver to understand what was being expressed. Most important for the present argument, members of face-to-face dyads had little specific memory of the other person's gestures (Rime & Schiaratura, 1991). All this suggests that the function of gesture, whatever it is, is relevant to the sender rather than the recipient of communications (Rime & Schiaratura, 1991). These movements may be important to the ability to communicate, although they are largely unconscious and are normally not explicitly taught to children learning to communicate.

So what, then, is the relation between these largely unconscious gestures and communication? Bernieri and Rosenthal (1991) argued that pleasant and successful social encounters are characterized by *interactional synchrony*—an interpersonal and intrapersonal coordination involving a high degree of patterning or synchronizing of behaviors. The phenomenon includes matching behaviors and postures, such as the mirroring of sitting positions or hand positions (LaFrance, 1982), as well as fluid synchrony, which includes rhythm, simultaneous movement, and smooth meshing of actions (Bernieri, Davis, Rosenthal, & Knee, 1991). This interactional synchrony, involving complex behaviors and their continual modification on the basis of social partners' responses, based on gesture, does not appear to relate closely to awareness. Interactional synchrony occurs very rapidly and apparently without any cognitive involvement.

Nor is it an activity requiring conscious acquisition. Condon and Sander (1974) demonstrated interactional synchrony in newborn infants, whose gestures were coordinated with their mothers' patterns of intonation. The evidence with infants, reviewed by Bernieri and Rosenthal (1991), showed that babies as young as a few days old synchronize their movements and their vocalizations to human speech (even if tape recorded or presented in a foreign language), whereas research has shown no synchrony to control stimuli such as traffic noise or rhythmic tapping (Cappella, 1981). Other research (Bernieri, Reznick, & Rosenthal, 1988) found that synchrony was higher between a mother and her own child than it was when the same adult interacted with an unfamiliar child. Cross-cultural replication suggests that this may be a generalized phenomenon of human infants and may indeed be an essential precursor to the development of language.

The earliest study of movement coordination in adult social interaction, both between individuals and within a single individual (Condon & Ogston, 1966), used film and tape to record and analyze interaction patterns. This study examined differences between control subjects and psychiatric patients, finding clear differences in their interactional patterns. Similar frame-by-frame analysis of film of natural social interactions among normal adults (Kendon, 1970) showed evidence of complex interactional patterns of which the participants had no awareness.

Bernieri and Rosenthal (1991) observed that, in adult social interaction, body movements are synchronized both with one's own speech and with the speech of others. More interesting, in terms of the noncognitive, nonconscious nature of this behavior, is evidence linking the level of observed interactional synchrony with perceived rapport. The extent of synchrony has been examined by comparing videotapes of interactive pairs with artificially constructed videotapes of pseudodyads—recordings of one person from each of two genuine dyads spliced together or juxtaposed using split-screen techniques. Bernieri (1988), using this technique, found that real dyads showed much higher levels of movement synchrony and behavior matching than did pseudodyads. Further, within the real pairs, self-ratings of rapport correlated highly with observed level of movement synchrony. This finding suggests that these complex and dynamically synchronized movements, which we have not been taught and are not aware of making, play a major role in the complex human activity of social communication.

Another technique for studying synchronous movement is the examination of highly degraded recordings of interactions. Bernieri et al. (1991) used mosaicing to mask fine motor cues and removed the soundtrack, but they still found that observers could identify levels of rapport and distinguish true dyads from pseudodyads. They suggested that because the mosaic process screens out the features relevant to assessing a person's emotional and attitudinal state (e.g., facial expression, fine motor movements, overall appearance), rapport must be a function of the interactional dynamics of a dyad, dynamics of which the dyad's members are not aware.

It is difficult to explain complex, interactive, and dynamic social skills in terms of overlearning, and it appears that a model of human decisions should be able to deal with these important behaviors. Again, the suggestion is that conscious thought is far less central to human behavior than many theorists seem to assume.

THEORIES OF HUMAN BEHAVIOR: PARTIALITY FOR COGNITIVE EXPLANATIONS

The fundamental argument of this book is that our current theories of human behavior are inadequate and that their inadequacy is based on an unwillingness to examine the assumption that cognition causes all but the most trivial of human actions. Understanding the causes of behavior is likely to require a fundamentally different approach from simply asking people what they are thinking, no matter how carefully we word the questions or how complicated the statistics we apply to the answers. Although behavioral explanations of human action are not currently fashionable (Hickey, 1994), a number of researchers continue to argue that it is unwise to overlook their value. Eifert and Plaud (1993), for example, argued that the cognitive–behavioral movement has led to an underemphasis on observable behavior and that this has obscured advances in behavioral theory. They pointed out that therapies increasingly concentrate on introspection to the exclusion of material reality and argued that "increased preoccupation with hypothesized inner processes will weaken the behavior therapy movement unless theories about private events are appropriately related to and integrated with basic behavioral concepts and research findings" (p.103).

It is understandable, in the current climate, that students and academics in general are not well informed about contemporary developments in behavioral theory, but basic behavioral research continues to develop and continues to be relevant to human behavior and to modern clinical psychology (Plaud & Vogeltanz, 1993). Eifert, Forsyth, and Schauss (1993) argued that many cognitive behaviorists seem to equate contemporary behavioral theory with its historical roots and are not aware that the field has developed.

It is also understandable, given the need for specialization and the impossibility of being thoroughly conversant with many different aspects of psychology, that "the limitations of early conditioning models and treatments have led many behavior therapists to abandon conditioning principles and replace them with loosely defined cognitive theories and treatments" (Eifert et al., 1993, p. 107). However, Eifert et al. (1993) argued that there was considerable potential for the development of a more strongly integrative approach that did not reject useful aspects of traditional behavioral approaches to human behavior. Although cognitive psychology may be in the ascendant, Eifert and Plaud (1993) compared it unfavorably to behavior theory, asking, "where ... have the conceptual foundations of the various cognitive–behavioral theories and treatments been adequately defined and elaborated on?" (p. 103).

Considering behavioral theories and noncognitive explanations of human action raises the question of the need for theories unique to *human* action. Models that emphasize cognition serve to emphasize our belief that human beings are different from other animals. However, animal-based evidence relates to many behaviors that we think of as uniquely human and that we believe must be based on complex cognitions beyond the capacities of other animals. For example, detailed work with primates (Mineka, 1987) as well as humans has indicated that vicarious learning, a capacity that contemporary social theorists consider to be necessarily cognitive in nature (Bandura, 1986), occurs in animals and may best be explained in classical conditioning terms. "Observers do not appear to be simply engaging in a social inference process" (Mineka, 1987, p. 107).

Massey (1993) suggested that psychology should reject the idea that people are fundamentally different from other animals and should reject any model of human activity that does not apply evenhandedly to animals "unless there is compelling evidence that the phenomena under investigation are particular to humans" (Massey, 1993, p. S97). If the observable actions of humans and other animals looked similar, argued Massey, then the most parsimonious explanation was that the actions had similar causes; furthermore, if a hypothesis was advanced to explain any action that occurred among both humans and other animals, then the same hypothesis should ideally explain both.

Because it is clear that nonhuman animals learn new behaviors, engage in social interactions, modify their actions in dynamic and sophisticated ways, and give every external impression of experiencing affect (Wasserman, 1993), it follows from Massey's argument that these require explanations that can be applied both to human and to nonhuman animals. Although the majority of psychologists seem prepared to accept that human beings' behavior is best explained in terms of expectations, beliefs, attitudes, and points of view, very few accept the existence of such hypothetical variables in the case of cats, dogs, and laboratory rats.

The obvious reply to this point, that humans have language and that this makes us fundamentally different from other animals (Hayes & Hayes, 1992), seems on the face of it a convincing one. However, if behaviors such as those previously listed can occur both in humans, who possess language, and in other animals, who do not, the possession of language is not fundamental to the possession of many complex skills.

Wasserman (1993) argued this point more strongly, citing empirical evidence to indicate that other animals, from pigeons to cetaceans, possess at least some of the basic skills required for language development, such as the ability to develop conceptual categories and an ability to use grammar. However, "most who advocate this cognitive approach have curiously found it easier to accept functional and structural parallels between human beings and digital computers than between human and nonhuman animals" (p. 222). It seems that many psychologists find the concept of underlying continuity between human and nonhuman animals unattractive, and a behavioral approach acknowledging our membership in the animal world meets considerable resistance.

CONCLUSION

Human behavior is complex, but like everything else, it is determined by material events. Recent developments in the theory of chaos (Glieck, 1987) are moving toward an understanding of highly complex dynamic systems, such as weather patterns and fluid turbulence. The theory of deterministic chaos (Schuster, 1989) deals with the persistent, ordered instability arising in highly complex physical systems. Human behavior is no more and no less than a complex physical system, and it may be that similar models, based entirely on observable events, will enable us to move toward a more scientific understanding of human behavior (Halasz, 1995; Mandel, 1995).

A corollary of the assumption that humans are different from other animals and are somehow free to behave in ways not subject to the same physical laws as the rest of the universe, is the view that people, unlike other animals, are rational, and that they are rational because, unlike other animals, they can think. In the following chapter I examine this more specific assumption of rationality, showing that the assumptions that rational thought is always appropriate and that humans are fundamentally different from other organisms because of a capacity for rational thought, cannot be sustained.

Chapter 7

Rationality: The Essential Human Characteristic?

I remember my grandmother saying ... 'When I think, I get confused.'
—Schnaitter (1987b, p. 57)

One attraction of theories that emphasize cognition is that they concentrate on an aspect of human nature that is, or at least seems, distinctly and uniquely human: our capacity for rational thought. It is obvious that even rather unintelligent humans can add and subtract, and so forth, whereas the most intelligent members of many other species seem unable to manage these feats.

The fact that humans seem to have an advanced capacity for ratiocination does not logically imply that we have a particularly advanced ability for thinking in general. Thinking is a broad term, used to describe a variety of phenomenological processes, including but not encompassed by those that adhere to the logic of rational thought. Nor does our ability in this aspect of thought imply that this skill is central to our behavior. However, the idea that rationality, and by extension thinking in general, is the particular greatness of the human species is an attractive one.

This chapter turns from the relation between cognition and behavior to a question at once broader and narrower, that of the position of rational thought in contemporary social and clinical psychology. Some current approaches to rationality are examined, and conceptual difficulties arising from definitional imprecision and from the mutual incompatibility of these approaches are pointed out. The more general assumption that the capacity for rational thought is centrally important in healthy human behavior is then discussed; although our society sets great store by rationality, the evidence suggests that rational thought, narrowly defined, is not always optimal.

The concept of rationality is central to several aspects of contemporary psychology. The influential cognitive–behavioral approaches to therapy (e.g., Ellis, 1962, 1993), discussed in earlier chapters, are based on the concept that dysfunctional emotional states necessarily arise from irrational thought processes. By contrast, cognitive models of depression and of optimism (e.g., Alloy & Clements, 1992) indicate that psychologically healthy thinking and rational thinking are not necessarily the same thing. A related area of research suggests that our ability to think rationally may actually be diminished by positive emotions (e.g., Mackie & Worth, 1991).

Also, there is the approach to rationality taken by the heuristics and biases literature (e.g., Kahneman, Slovic, & Tversky, 1982). This identifies irrational distortions in normal human decision making, suggesting that human beings are not particularly good at thinking rationally. This research suggests that irrational thinking may be a normal characteristic of human judgments, providing useful heuristics for simplifying an overly complicated world. Thus, this line of research suggests that irrational thinking may be normal and useful, contradicting arguments that it is necessarily depressogenic.

RATIONALITY IN SOCIAL AND CLINICAL PSYCHOLOGY

Rational Living: Cognitive–Behavioral Therapies

A discussion of the rhetoric of rational thought in psychology should perhaps begin with cognitive–behavioral therapies based on the view that healthy human beings are essentially rational. Ellis' rational–emotive therapy (RET) model (e.g., Ellis, 1984, 1993), for example, holds that human unhappiness is caused by adherence to one or more irrational beliefs, that the replacement of these beliefs by more rational ones will lead to psychological well-being, and that the appropriate method for achieving this replacement is primarily through cognitive rather than behavioral means. Ellis' model maintains a strong group of adherents (e.g., Barnard & DiGiuseppe, 1989), even though its theoretical and empirical bases have been rejected by many writers (e.g., Coyne & Gotlib, 1986; Cramer & Fong, 1991; Cramer & Kupshik, 1993; Eschenroeder, 1982; Holt & Lee, 1989; Mahoney, 1977; Meichenbaum, 1977; Wolpe, 1993), and its sociopolitical implications have been questioned (e.g., Prilleltensky, 1989).

An early review of empirical studies using RET (DiGiuseppe, Miller, & Trexler, 1977) concluded that RET was no better than convincing placebo interventions. Despite theoretical developments (e.g., Ellis, 1984, 1993), several more recent empirical reviews (Engels, Garnefski, & Diekstra, 1993; Gossette & O'Brien, 1992, 1993) have also shown little evidence for RET's effectiveness, either with adults or with children. Engels et al. (1993) found RET to be superior to no treatment, but none of the reviews indicated RET to be superior to placebo or to behaviorally oriented treatments.

Haaga and Davison (1993) recently concluded, on the subject of RET, that "its professional impact thus far exceeds its scientific status" (p. 215). They criticized RET outcome research on a number of grounds, including lack of definition of irrational beliefs, use of invalid and unreliable scales, poor follow-up, high attrition, and overreliance on self-reports and singular outcome measures. More recently, the same group addressed the "apparent gap between RET's clinical and scientific reputation" (Kendall, Haaga, Ellis, Bernard, DiGuiseppe, & Kassinove, 1995, p. 170) and argued that researchers have failed to take theoretical developments into account when evaluating treatments.

The highly influential theory of depression developed by Beck (e.g., Beck, 1963, 1976, 1984, 1991; Beck, Rush, Shaw, & Emery, 1979) has similarities to that of Ellis. However, as discussed in earlier chapters, the basis of Beck's argument is not that irrational cognitions cause depression but that irrationally negative cognitions (defined as dysfunctional automatic thoughts) are an integral part of the depressive condition. Beck has argued that biased cognitions are activated by some actual cause, which may be an aspect or combination of biological, genetic, environmental, or personality factors (Beck, 1991), but that these cognitions, once activated, then serve to maintain the depression.

Although Beck's theoretical analysis is more sophisticated than Ellis', the therapeutic implications are in many ways the same. It is argued that therapy should focus on dysfunctional or illogical cognitions, and changing cognitions is seen as the appropriate way to alleviate depression (e.g., Beck, 1976).

A high rate of negative cognitions is a frequent characteristic of depression (e.g., Hollon & Beck, 1979), and it is unquestionable that interventions based on Beck's model produce good therapeutic results (Dobson, 1989). What is open to question, as discussed in chapter 4, however, is the mechanism by which these therapeutic improvements occur (Haaga et al., 1991). The specific aim of this section is to question the assumptions first that negative and irrational cognitions are either a cause (e.g., Ellis, 1984) or a maintaining factor (e.g., Beck, 1976) of depression and second that the cognitions characteristic of depression are necessarily inaccurate or illogical.

Prospective research (e.g., Lewinsohn, Steinmetz, Larson, & Franklin, 1981; Silverman, Silverman, & Eardley, 1984) has shown that negative cognitions do not appear as precursors to depression but arise at the same time as the affective and behavioral aspects of depressive episodes, casting doubt on Ellis' assumption that they play a causal role. Beck (1991) did not argue for a causal role for cognition but rather claimed that the presence of particular schemata and personality characteristics will predispose individuals to develop depressive symptoms, including negative cognitions. However, the review by Haaga et al. (1991) found no evidence that people who later develop depression can be identified a priori on the basis of any personality type or classes of schemata.

Furthermore, depressed people are exposed to an objectively more negative environment than nondepressed people are (Marcus & Nardone, 1992), suggesting that the negative cognitions experienced are not necessarily incorrect. Depressed people have more aversive personal experiences than others (e.g., Gotlib & Robinson, 1982; Howes & Hokanson, 1979). They tend to associate with other depressed people (Rosenblatt & Greenberg, 1991) or those who reflect their own negative perceptions of themselves (Swann, Stein-Seroussi, & Giesler, 1992); they have fewer and less pleasant social encounters (Nezlek, Imbrie, & Shean, 1994) and experience more social rejection and avoidance than the nondepressed (Burchill & Stiles, 1988; Segrin & Abramson, 1994; Strack & Coyne, 1983; Swann, Wenzlaff, Krull, & Pelham, 1992).

Thus, the apparently excessive negative cognitions may be not irrational, but reasonable and accurate reflections of a negative context. It also appears that the depressed may not have a completely negative self-view, but may be capable of realistic perception of at least some positive aspects of themselves (e.g., Pelham, 1991). This suggests that negative judgments may result from something other than a generalized internal distortion of reality. Arguments and evidence such as these suggest that the alleviation of depression might best be achieved, not by changing the individual's thought patterns, but by changing the negative context that maintains the depression. The argument that depression and anxiety arise from or are maintained by inappropriate or irrational cognitive interpretations of neutral environmental stimuli is not supported by current evidence (Eschenroeder, 1982). Sampson (1981) and, more recently, Prilleltensky (1989, 1990b) have criticized cognitive–behavioral psychology in general for what they consider to be an overemphasis on self-reports of internal events and a tendency to treat actual events in the real world as of peripheral relevance.

Although Beck's model is the most influential of the cognition-centered views of dysfunctional emotion, it does not seem as successful an explanatory model as it is a framework for intervention. Little evidence supports the notion that depression results from irrational processing of information or that changing information-processing strategies is the mechanism by which therapies for depression work (Eschenroeder, 1982). Furthermore, the evidence suggests that the assumption that a failure of rational thought is the basic problem of depressed people cannot be sustained.

Depressive Realism, Unjustifiable Optimism, and the Illusion of Control

The concept that depressives' thought processes, where they differ from those of nondepressed people, are necessarily irrational has been challenged by evidence for depressive realism (e.g., Alloy & Abramson, 1979). This work is complemented by research showing that an unjustifiably optimistic bias may be characteristic of the normal judgments of psychologically healthy individuals (Taylor & Brown, 1988). Depressed people may, at least in some ways, have an accurate view of the world, whereas the judgments of nondepressed people may be systematically biased. This hypothesis challenges the concept that impaired perceptions of reality are an essential ingredient of depression and other psychological disturbances and the related concept that treatment of depression will be effective if it corrects faulty perceptions (Ackermann & DeRubeis, 1991).

Two reviews of the depressive–realism hypothesis (Ackermann & DeRubeis, 1991; Dobson & Franche, 1989) pointed out the need to distinguish discrepancy between the responses of depressed and nondepressed individuals on the one hand and actual distortion of judgment by either group on the other. Much of the research finding differences between samples did not address the question of whether it is the normal sample, the depressives, or both whose judgments are at variance with objective reality.

For example, Matt, Vazquez, and Campbell (1992) found that depressives were more likely to remember negative stimuli, whereas nonclinical samples were more likely to remember positive stimuli. In a similar vein, social-skill research (e.g., Kuiper & MacDonald, 1982; Lewinsohn, Mischel, Chaplin, & Barton, 1980) indicates that depressives' judgments of their own interpersonal skills are closer to the judgments of independent observers than are the self-perceptions of normal individuals. Although this research demonstrates group differences, it says nothing about the rationality of either group. The definition of rational or correct responses in many social situations is a matter of opinion rather than objective reality, and thus differing responses are not necessarily more or less correct (Eiser, 1994).

However, other research allows people's perceptions to be compared with an independently verifiable standard of accuracy. The phenomenon of illusion of control, originally proposed by Langer (1975), provides a context for much of this research. It is argued, on the basis of substantial evidence, that normal individuals are characterized by an inaccurate perception referred to as the "illusion" of control, the subjective impression that they have more control over events in their environment than is objectively the case.

Several studies that compared the responses of mildly depressed and nondepressed college students (e.g., Alloy & Abramson, 1979; Layne, 1983) indicated that depressed people seemed to have less of this illusion than others: They were better at recognizing situations in which there was no contingency between their behavior and events in the environment. Rosenfarb, Burker, Morris, and Cush (1993) obtained similar results with a sample of clinically depressed students: Depressed students were more likely to respond to changes in contingencies during an analog task than were nondepressed students, who tended to persist with an explicitly stated rule, even when contingencies had changed. Although some researchers (e.g., Bryson, Doan, & Pasquali, 1984) have failed to confirm this effect, other similar work (e.g., Dobson & Pusch, 1995) has supported the concept of depressive realism.

A review of studies involving judgment of contingency of control (Dobson & Franche, 1989) concluded that they generally showed depressed people's judgments to be closer to objective reality than were judgments of nondepressed people. Dobson and Franche's review also covered research using feedback on task performance (e.g., Dennard & Hokanson, 1986) and judgments of interpersonal behavior (e.g., Gotlib & Meltzer, 1987); findings in these areas are less clear-cut but generally support the hypothesis that depressives make realistic judgments whereas others show an unsubstantiated positive bias. Depressives are also less likely than nondepressed people to exhibit a positive bias when making judgments about themselves, relative to making judgments about others (Alloy & Ahrens, 1987; Vallone, Griffin, Lin, & Ross, 1990).

Much of this research uses artificial tasks that may not be personally meaningful to participants and investigates students with mild levels of depression. Coyne (1994) argued that this places the focus on the "wrong phenomena in the wrong population" (p. 30) for the development of an understanding of clinical depression. Ackermann and DeRubeis (1991) have hypothesized that the depressive realism effect may be specific to mildly dysphoric individuals and may not occur in the clinically depressed. However, those studies including severely depressed patients (e.g., Golin, Terrell, Weitz, & Drost, 1979) have obtained similar results to those obtained with mildly dysphoric individuals, and a review (Vredenburg, Flett, & Krames, 1993) concluded that few theoretically relevant differences in research outcomes exist when research with dysphoric students is compared with that conducted with clinical populations. Dobson and Franche (1989) argued that, taken together, the evidence is sufficient to support the claim that realism, not irrationality, is characteristic of the judgments of depressed individuals.

Numerous other investigators (e.g., Kuiper & MacDonald, 1982; Layne, 1983; Lewinsohn et al., 1980; Martin, Abramson, & Alloy, 1984; Vestre & Caulfield, 1986) have confirmed the notion that all people may exhibit illogical or systematically biased cognitions, and in some circumstances nondepressed people show greater degrees of distortion than depressed respondents. In addition, Benassi and Mahler (1985) showed that mildly depressed students will react in the same way as a control population under some circumstances but not others. In a related piece of research, Meyer and Hokanson (1985) found that depressed people are capable of varying their interpersonal behavior according to context, to the same extent as do nondepressed people. This finding again suggests that a specifically depressogenic context, rather than any enduring personal or cognitive characteristics of the individual, may be most important in maintaining depression.

The research that compares depressed and nondepressed respondents is generally cross-sectional in nature and thus does not reflect on the direction of causation between rationality and depression. However, evidence from mood-induction research provides support for the hypothesis that depressed mood functions to enhance rational decision making, rather than that an enhanced capacity for rational thought causes depression.

Alloy, Abramson, and Viscusi (1981), using a mood-induction strategy to produce mild, transient depression in normal subjects, found a significant reduction in illusion of control and suggested that this showed accurate and rational decision making to be a consequence, not a cause of depressed mood. This, in turn, tends to weaken the more general view that emotional states arise as a direct result of cognitive states (Coyne & Gotlib, 1986). Taylor and Brown (1988), however, argued that the reverse is not necessarily the case. Unrealistic thought may not be just a consequence of positive mood but, rather, may be a prerequisite for positive emotional health, including the ability to work successfully, to care for others, and to cope with negative or threatening information.

Recently, Haaga and Beck (1995) addressed the apparent contradiction between cognitive-distortion-based models of depression and evidence such as that reviewed here. They acknowledged that "cognitive distortions are not an inevitable feature of depressive thinking nor unheard of among nondepressed people. Beck's theoretical writings have sometimes implied a generality of depressive distortion and (implicitly) nondepressive accuracy that probably cannot be sustained" (p. 45). They also argued that the crucial issue was not one of whether depressives or nondepressed people seemed more rational in artificial laboratory settings, but a broader and more complex question. Depressives, they argued, might not be any less logical than others, but they were characterized by other important cognitive biases, such as a tendency to perseverate with nonfunctional patterns of behavior (although the findings of Rosenfarb et al., 1993, contradict this conclusion) and an inability to generate behavioral alternatives or to explore problems creatively. Thus, Haaga and Beck (1995) argued that an acknowledgment of depressive realism served to encourage a more sophisticated and complex examination of the biases of depressed individuals.

Optimism, Realism, and Pessimism: Variations on a Theme

Although Taylor and Brown (1988) suggested that the person with stronger optimistic illusions would cope better with challenging events, possibly by persisting with problem-solving efforts, it seems equally plausible that an optimistic bias might interfere with appropriate decision making (Block & Colvin, 1994; Mackie & Worth, 1991). Unjustified optimism could lead to failure to take a problem seriously and thus to a deficit in coping actions or preventive behavior, which might have the potential to exacerbate a serious problem, to increase risk of disease, or otherwise to result in the selection of less than optimal behavior (e.g., Lee, 1989a; Weinstein, 1989).

Arising from the depressive realism and unrealistic optimism literature have been a number of attempts to refine or clarify the concept. Several mutually incompatible hypotheses have been proposed, to define the circumstances under which realistic or optimistic thought might occur or to specify when these are appropriate strategies.

Dolinski, Gromski, and Zawisza (1987), for example, argued that the optimistic bias may be specific to events that are potential rather than real and also that it may apply to events that are familiar and individual-specific rather than to those that are unfamiliar and affect entire communities. With a survey conducted one month after the Chernobyl nuclear reactor accident, they examined Polish students' perceptions of a variety of risks, including the risk of suffering from radiation exposure. The expected unrealistic optimism was obtained for a number of hypothetical threats, including being involved in an accident and suffering a heart attack. However, subjects rated the risk to themselves of suffering ill effects of radiation significantly higher than they did the risk to their fellow students. Dolinski et al. (1987) argued that this might have been because the event was real, not hypothetical, that the danger had already occurred and that the preventive strategies available to subjects were not perceived as particularly effective. Thus, the protective belief that they could take action to protect themselves (Weinstein, 1993) was not relevant. Alternatively, they argued, the unfamiliarity of the threat may have meant that subjects were unable to make use of existing self-serving schemata.

In a more general review, Weinstein (1989) argued that optimism was not universal, although it seemed to be more common than pessimism in normal subjects. He argued that optimism was strongest for events of which the respondents had little experience, for low-probability events, for events which were, or at least appeared to be, controllable by personal action, and for negative events (such as certain diseases) which manifested themselves at an early, benign stage of development. Events such as these, he argued, were seen as potentially controllable or avoidable, and thus people believed that they would be able to avoid them.

By contrast, Norem and Cantor (1986) argued that negative biases were widespread. They hypothesized a *defensive pessimism*: the use of low or negative expectations to cope with anxiety about future events. Dewberry, Ing, James, Nixon, and Richardson (1990) studied nondepressed college students and found defensive pessimism, but only with relation to events about which the subjects were anxious, such as examinations. A second study (Dewberry & Richardson, 1990) showed that situationally induced anxiety, again relating to examinations, seemed to reduce optimism about events in general. This line of research suggests that negative thoughts may in fact be adaptive in some situations, in that anxiety and pessimism about a future event may motivate a person to behave in ways that increase the chances of positive outcomes.

Schwarzer (1994) argued for the existence of defensive optimism, which he distinguished from functional optimism. His argument was that defensive optimism, an implicit belief in one's invulnerability, reduced one's motivation to take preventive actions and thus increased the chances of negative outcomes. This, clearly, is quite a different concept from Norem and Cantor's defensive pessimism. Both are defenses in the sense that both may reduce anxiety, but Norem and Cantor's concept of this defense is that it motivates effort, whereas Schwarzer's concept of defense has the opposite effect. Schwarzer's functional optimism is a different concept again, the idea that effort is generally rewarded and that, by taking action, one will experience positive outcomes. Wallston (1994) described yet another way of looking at "good" and "bad" optimism: He distinguished between the cautious and the naive optimist, arguing again that the one will act to maintain a positive state of affairs or to avoid problems, whereas the other will not. Taylor and Gollwitzer (1995) also described a variation on the two-types-of-optimism theme, arguing that healthy individuals are capable of switching between two different mindsets: a deliberative mindset, used when deciding what to do, which is immune to positive illusions, and an implemental mindset, used during action, which experiences illusions. All these variations, however, have been proposed in the vaguest of terms and suffer from the problems discussed earlier—the invocation of further hypothetical constructs, when one's existing collection is shown to be inadequate, is not an appropriate approach to a clearer understanding of the phenomenon under question.

Scheier and Carver (1992) argued, along similar lines to Taylor and Brown (1988), that unjustifiable optimism is a desirable characteristic: It helps individuals to cope with the vicissitudes of life and is a factor in positive physical and psychological health. They did, however, make the point that unrealistic optimism might only be of value when combined with the view that it is individual effort that keeps one in a superior position. Persons who held this particular combination of views, they argued, would be likely to persevere with productive and health-enhancing strategies until they succeeded, and thus their beliefs would become self-fulfilling prophecies. This view clearly has similarities with Schwarzer's (1994) concepts of defensive and functional optimism as well as with Wallston's (1994) classification of cautious and naive optimists.

The problem with all this, of course, is the same as the problem with dysfunctional thoughts. None of these writers has offered any independent definitions of good versus bad optimism. Whether optimism is good, bad, or indifferent seems to depend on its outcomes, and thus a circular line of reasoning is set up once more.

Optimistic Illusions and Mental Health

Although illusion of control is not necessarily the same as unrealistic optimism (McKenna, 1993), the concepts are related in that both involve a positive distortion of rational thinking. In support of a connection between illusions and mental health, Alloy and Clements (1992) conducted a prospective study that showed that the strength of respondents' illusions of control predicted their later ability to cope with negative events without becoming depressed. This might suggest that an irrationally positive outlook on life will protect individuals against reactive depression. It derives, however, from a small-scale pilot study, which assessed a nonclinical student sample over a single month, during which major life events were fairly unlikely to occur. Thus, the results, although suggestive, are by no means definitive. Whether unrealistic optimism would really help or hinder in coping with seriously challenging life events is an issue yet to be addressed.

Positive mood, and the irrational judgmental processes that are argued to accompany it, may not always be desirable. Positive moods seem to interfere with critical thinking, making happy people more readily persuasible (Mackie & Worth, 1991). A review of the evidence (Schwarz, Bless, & Bohner, 1991) suggested that negative moods tended to lead a person to more rational, analytical reasoning, whereas positive moods were associated with a more creative, inferential cognitive approach. If a negative mood state enhances one's ability to think rationally and analytically, it could be an adaptive response to negative environmental conditions. Thus, it is possible to argue that negative mood may, at least in some circumstances, be a functional response to a negative context, serving to enhance the person's ability to analyze the situation and seek solutions.

Early research on the influence of positive emotions on cognitive functioning tended to emphasize disruptive effects, particularly on analytical reasoning (Schwarz & Bless, 1991), and seemed to be based on the assumption that judgments made under the influence of any emotion, whether positive or negative, were always wrong. However, the relation between positive emotion and cognition seems to be more complex than simply one of interference. The evidence reviewed by Schwarz et al. (1991), suggesting that the cognitive processes of happy people are flexible and creative, suggests that good moods, like bad ones, will enhance cognitive functioning but only in some situations.

Petty, Gleicher, and Baker (1991) argued that affect, regardless of its valence, can influence attitudes by motivating the person to think about the subject and by influencing the types of thought as well as by affecting information-processing activity. Forgas (1994), discussing the role of emotion in social judgments, argued that the extent to which affect influences judgment depends on the way in which that judgment is formed. Judgments about familiar stimuli or judgments motivated by a desire for a specific outcome (Kunda, 1990) are unlikely to be influenced by affect, whereas judgments that are less connected to abiding personal concerns and that are developed at the time they are expressed will be influenced by momentary affective state. Whatever the mechanism, it does appear that happy people may be more gullible and more prone to influence than depressed people, suggesting that there may be at least some situations in which happiness is a disadvantage and others in which it is desirable (Petty et al., 1991).

Irrational or illogical thought processes are not an exclusive or even a necessary characteristic of psychopathology. Rather, under certain conditions, both normal and abnormal individuals may exhibit logical or illogical cognitions. Furthermore, there may be some situations in which a narrowly logical, analytical approach is most adaptive and others in which a more flexible and heuristic approach is more effective.

Irrationality alone can certainly not be regarded as a necessary or sufficient cause of emotional distress (Rachman, 1983). On the other hand, it seems that the wholesale acceptance of positively biased thought processes as the key to good psychological health (Taylor & Brown, 1988) may be as problematic as the equally wholehearted acceptance of rational thought as the path to personal happiness (Ellis, 1984).

Rational Thought in the Biases and Heuristics Literature

The biases and heuristics literature (e.g., Kahneman et al., 1982) argues that some types of irrationality result inevitably from the decision making of normal human beings. Research over several decades has identified a number of common decision-making strategies that can lead to judgments that do not accord with a formal, logical analysis (e.g., Baron, 1988; Kahneman & Tversky, 1973; Tversky & Kahneman, 1981).

The general argument of this literature is that normal human decision making is based on simplified, illogical rules of thumb. Under some circumstances, these decision-making heuristics produce answers that are demonstrably irrational. This research has generally used specific, artificial experimental tasks, and the extent to which findings can be generalized to natural decision making has generated debate. Nisbett, Krantz, Jepson, and Kunda (1983), for example, argued that illogical strategies only occurred in particular types of tasks and showed that, with certain other types of task, subjects use heuristics based consciously on statistical principles. Thus, they concluded, it was not that people were incapable of formally rational thought but merely that under some circumstances they chose not to use it.

Hogarth (1981) made the point that the judgmental heuristics that produce "wrong" responses in artificial situations may be functional in natural settings, in which decision making is an iterative process with scope for correction. In a similar vein, Frisch and Jones (1993) pointed out that making a decision that will maximize desirable consequences might be a better criterion for judging the goodness of decisions than conformity with a formal statistical model. Thus, decisions that look wrong at a formal level may be the most adaptive in practical terms.

Although arguments such as these seek to deal with the phenomenon by changing the criterion of correctness, they do not deny that the use of logically indefensible heuristics is a characteristic of normal human judgment in at least some situations. The body of evidence from this particular research area suggests that irrational thinking, in a formal, statistical sense, is commonplace and may even be valuable in some contexts. This conclusion is not incompatible with the concept that illusions and other irrational thought processes may be important in the maintenance of positive psychological health but is clearly difficult to reconcile with the arguments from the clinical models presented earlier, that irrational thinking is necessarily depressogenic.

PSYCHOLOGICAL THEORIES AND FAITH IN RATIONALITY

Clearly, even a brief review invalidates the simple notion that all irrational thought is the same and will necessarily lead to emotional disorders. The literature outlined so far is connected in the sense that it deals with rationality and with human social behavior. However, the models have obvious incompatibilities. It is clearly impossible to argue simultaneously that failures of rational, analytical thought are essential aspects of depression (Beck, 1991), are the result of positive moods (Bower, 1991), are essential prerequisites for mental health (Kendall, 1992), and are an inevitable component of normal human problem solving (Kahneman et al., 1982).

These inconsistencies arise to some extent from differing definitions of rational thought, although the problem is not only one of semantics. To Ellis (1993), rational thoughts are compatible with a healthy adaptation to the vicissitudes of life, whereas to Tversky and Kahneman (1981) they are problem-solving strategies that accord with formal laws of probability.

Abramson and Alloy (1981) pointed out a need to distinguish between erroneous, irrational, and maladaptive cognitions. One response to this has been to replace the word irrational with dysfunctional (e.g., Ellis, 1993) and leave the rest of the argument intact. However, a change in nomenclature does not solve the basic definitional problem. Depression, runs the argument, is caused by dysfunctional thinking. Therefore, the thinking of depressed people must be dysfunctional. Furthermore, it must be the type of dysfunctional thinking that causes depression. Because negative emotions must be caused by bad thoughts, any thought held by a person experiencing negative emotions must be a bad thought. In this way, a circular, nonfalsifiable argument is set up in which thoughts are defined as dysfunctional according to their association with depression, and depression is defined as arising from dysfunctional thoughts.

Rorer (1989) proposed that irrational beliefs, in the RET sense, can be defined independent of their outcomes. He proposed that the term *irrational belief* should refer to any evaluation derived from nonempirical premises and stated in absolutist language. Although this may remove the circularity problem, as a definitive description of the class of belief that causes depression it is inadequate. There are many beliefs, for example those associated with the illusion of control, that fit this definition but are known not to be associated with depression. The Ten Commandments serve as another example of what Rorer (1989) called irrational beliefs, and it is difficult to sustain the argument that any person who chooses to follow the Ten Commandments will necessarily suffer from psychological dysfunction.

An unwillingness to challenge the central principle, that bad cognitions are the root cause of depression and other human problems, combined with a lack of definition of useful and harmful cognitions, leads to the confusing and mutually incompatible collection of points of view that has so far been advanced. In a discussion of this issue, Lopes (1991) raised the question of why psychologists are concerned to such an extent with the rationality of human thought. A great deal of applied research, according to Lopes (1991), reflects an uncritical acceptance of the equivalence of rational and good, and of the concept that normal, or at least psychologically healthy, humans behave irrationally only in exceptional situations.

In the subculture of psychological research, it seems perfectly reasonable to ask a question such as that posed in the title of a recent publication: "Is teenage sexual behavior rational?" (Loewenstein & Furstenberg, 1991). The answer in this particular case, as one might have guessed, was no. Why ask the question about teenage sexual behavior? The underlying assumption seems to be that most behavior is rational and that particular subject groups (e.g., teenagers) and behaviors (e.g., sexual activity) are interesting and unusual in that they are likely to deviate from the dictates of rational thought.

Such work stands in stark contrast to research based on the assumption that almost all human thought is irrational and, by implication, wrong. On this topic, Christensen-Szalanski and Beach (1984) argued that there was a bias in the heuristics and biases literature, such that studies showing illogical decision making among subjects were cited more often than those showing logical decision making; they suggested that this bias tended to support a false perception that humans' inability to think rationally was an indisputable fact. This contention has been challenged more recently by Robins and Craik (1993), who concluded that the evidence for a citation bias is fairly weak. However, it does still appear that research demonstrating biased decision making has been more widely disseminated, has appeared in more prestigious journals, and has received more attention from the general public than research demonstrating accurate judgments.

Empirical demonstrations of irrationality are inherently more interesting, perhaps because more unexpected, than demonstrations of accurate decision making. Lopes (1991), however, analyzed the rhetoric of the literature on heuristics and biases, putting the argument that it was based on thinly disguised value judgments: Irrational or illogical thinking is necessarily inferior to that which conforms with probability theory. Lopes argued that findings from artificial laboratory situations have been overgeneralized to reach the conclusion that our everyday ability is deficient: "human incompetence is presented as a fact" (Lopes, 1991, p. 67). She presented an alternative interpretation, pointing out that, in most problems of the types studied in this literature, heuristic processing and rational calculation based on formal logic give the same answer. Thus, heuristic strategies generally work in real life, and when they do not, the iterative nature of decision making allows most incorrect decisions to be identified and corrected before inalterable negative consequences arise. The implication of this is that, even if people's decisions are frequently not narrowly logical, they are still generally functional.

A slightly different approach has been taken by Kunda (1990), who argued that human reasoning is guided not simply by logic and a motivation for accuracy but also by a motivation to arrive at particular, personally desirable conclusions. He argued that, in normal decision making, these two motivations work together: People arrive at the conclusions they want, but only if they can construct reasonable justifications for them. Kunda (1990) argued that human beings seem to value an illusion of objectivity, despite their use of motivated reasoning to reach conclusions that are personally desirable.

CONCLUSION

In attempting to reconcile the confusing and contradictory literature on rational thought, it may be useful to consider the proposition that thought content, whether rational or irrational, may not be the central determinant of behavior and of mood that many contemporary theorists assume (Coyne, 1982).

Argyle (1991), arguing against a primarily rationalist view of human behavior, put the view that rational-thought explanations of human social behavior miss much of importance. He criticized "the hard-line version of cognitive social psychology [that] sees social behaviour and judgements as a kind of rational problem-solving, performed by computer-like processes in the head" (p. 161) and argued that social behavior in particular could not be understood without considering emotional and contextual variables. "A number of applied problems can be tackled better by recognition of the non-cognitive components" (p. 176). In a similar vein, several authors (e.g., Hineline, 1992; Mixon, 1991; Morris, 1991) have argued that contextualist theories, with less emphasis on the specific content of hypothetical intraindividual variables and more on the interplay of persons and contexts, could be more fruitful than the mechanistic, linear models of cognitivism.

It is clear, however, that arguments of this nature go largely unheeded. Baer, Wolf and Risley (1987) suggested that psychologists have a culturally acquired tendency to find mentalistic explanations of human behavior reinforcing, but there is no compelling reason to assume that this tendency is specific to psychologists.

One attraction of theories that emphasize logic and rational thought is that they concentrate on the one aspect of human nature that is, or at least seems, distinctly and uniquely human. Models of personal distress or emotional dysfunction that identify irrational or otherwise faulty thinking as the fundamental problem confirm our cultural stereotype that a well-adjusted, normal person is primarily a thinker.

There also seems a powerful tendency to favor explanatory models which regard the mind as something special, something separate from and other than the physical world (Hineline, 1992). Prilleltensky (1990b) pointed out that one implication of this approach was a tendency to see psychological problems as residing inside the person, rather than resulting from a complex interaction of personal, social, and environmental factors. The implication is that the individual should be the only focus of research and therapy. In this way, social conditions that might maintain human problems tended to be ignored by mainstream psychology.

It could be argued that clients may feel more comfortable with a cognitive –behavioral model than with a behavioral one. An approach that is congruent with the client's point of view may be the most productive way to proceed, given that the aim of therapy is to assist a person with a problem rather than to answer a theoretical question. However, theoretical questions are not purely of academic interest. As I have shown in earlier chapters, they are important practically. The inadequacy of definitions and lack of real distinction between constructs make the theories unscientific; it means that if a change occurs, it is difficult to identify exactly how, and it means that improvements in techniques will only happen in an ad hoc fashion, rather than through enhanced understanding.

Another potential problem of thought-centered systems of explanation for human behavior is that, by assuming a discontinuity between ourselves and other animals (Massey, 1993), we may fall into the trap of assuming that we are something other than other animals, something more than complex physical systems, within which every action has a physical cause.

The questions that are previous to that of whether rational thought is good, bad or irrelevant are those of identifying the circumstances under which thought affects behavior and those under which it does not, and those of identifying the type and extent of other, noncognitive influences on human behavior. A conclusion that may be drawn from the unsatisfactory disorder of this single area of contemporary psychology is that conscious thought, in the sense of statements about internal processes that can be articulated verbally, may well be less essential to behavior than popular theories have tended to assume.

Chapter 8

The Politics of Cognition: On the Fatal Attractiveness of Cognitive Models

> ... solutions for human predicaments are to be found within the self, leaving the social order unaffected.
>
> —Prilleltensky (1989, p. 796)

It is clear that criticism of cognitive models of human behavior is a minority activity. The cognitive paradigm continues to enjoy hegemony across the entire subject matter of psychology and is widely regarded as a major advance on previous theoretical approaches (e.g., Sperry, 1993, 1995). Theories based on this paradigm are all characterized by a reliance on the concept that cognition is central to human nature and that the best way to begin the complex task of understanding and helping other people is by focusing on conscious thought.

This chapter examines the question of why psychology persists with an individualistic and cognitive approach to the virtual exclusion of all alternatives, despite repeated argument and considerable evidence that it is less than adequate as an explanation of human action. Suggestions that cognition is not necessarily the cause of behavior and subjective experience (e.g., Zajonc, 1984) are generally met with strong and emotional criticism (e.g., Parrott & Sabini, 1989; Tsal, 1985). Not only does psychology focus almost entirely on the individual, but it restricts itself, within those individuals, almost entirely to subjective experience.

INDIVIDUALISM

Psychology, if it has any coherence at all, may be characterized as an approach to human behavior that focuses on the individual and ignores the broader social context. Indeed, "from its inception a hundred years ago, ... psychology has been quintessentially a psychology of the individual organism, a characteristic that ... has severely and adversely affected psychology's contribution to human welfare" (Sarason, 1981, p. 827).

In an article reviewing the historical roots of social psychology, Sarason (1981) argued that it was impossible to understand individual human beings without first understanding the social and historical contexts in which they lived. Psychology, he argued, would never be able to make a useful contribution to society until it moved away from a focus on the personal and the narrowly interpersonal to consider broader issues.

More recently, Kipnis (1994) took up this point, arguing that the discipline of psychology has the potential to focus on broad social issues but that it has deliberately chosen to focus on the individual. Kipnis argued that the value accorded to experimentation within the culture of psychological research and the emphasis on tight experimental control in artificial settings has served to develop a focus on the individual human being, existing more or less in a vacuum, at the expense of social reality.

However, and despite repeated calls for psychology to broaden its awareness of sociohistorical influences (e.g., Prilleltensky, 1992; Sampson, 1977, 1994), psychologists have traditionally shied away from an analysis that moves beyond the intrapersonal or the narrowly interpersonal (Prilleltensky, 1990a; Sarason, 1981). Bevan and Kessel (1994) argued that both the broad context of our society and the narrower one of academia have tended to promote competitiveness, alienation from wider social concerns, and a focus on technology rather than on creative solutions to real-world problems. Thus, we are generally not encouraged to look beyond the individual to understand his or her problems.

In a similar vein, Kipnis (1994) stressed that social psychology, historically, has generally served to support rather than to challenge social institutions. "For the most part, research applications that validate the existing social order are supported" (p. 169). The emphasis on the individual and the need for individual change distracts attention from social and physical conditions. Prilleltensky (1989) argued along similar lines that psychologists tended to ignore sociopolitical and ideological influences on human behavior. This lack of attention to ideology, he argued, might arise in part because psychologists, in the main, belonged to the more privileged groups of their own privileged societies. Personal comfort might make it easy for psychologists to overlook the fact that psychology, as it is currently practiced, supports the existing social order and all its inequities. In doing so, it virtually ignores the majority of the world's population (Malpass, 1988) and the most pressing of the world's problems (Morf, 1994).

Kipnis (1994) took this point further, arguing that personal comfort and well-being encouraged a perception among psychologists and other influential professionals that twentieth-century Western society was a comfortable, pleasant, and desirable one. Thus, it may be understandable that our research efforts focus on helping other people to fit into this same society, rather than seeking to change it or, less radically, to understand the relations between individual behavior and social systems.

COGNITIVISM

A focus on the individual leads, seemingly inevitably, to a focus on cognition. The implicit ideology of cognitive psychology was described by Prilleltensky (1989): "A pervasive dichotomy between the individual and society is observed in psychology .... The immediate ideological benefit derived from such a dichotomy is that the individual is studied as an asocial and ahistorical being whose life vicissitudes are artificially disconnected from the wider sociopolitical context. Consequently, solutions for human predicaments are to be found within the self, leaving the social order unaffected" (p. 796).

Sampson (1981) argued that cognitive models reduce our subject matter from the entirety of human activity to the study of the subjective and individual. The individual's subjective experience of the world becomes the subject matter; this both rests on and underlies an unexamined assumption that the answer to personal distress is not to act to alter reality but to change cognitions to make them more consistent with the status quo. "In substituting thought for action ... cognitivism veils the objective sources and bases of social life and relegates individual potency to the inner world of mental gymnastics " (Sampson, 1981, p. 735). Thus, according to Sampson, psychology is based on and maintains an assumption that the job of the individual is to adjust as successfully as possible to the real world.

Gergen (1989) made a similar point about the broader field of social psychology. He argued that "the retreat to cognitive explanations" served to reduce real events to their cognitive, subjective representations. In such a context, real events are not perceived as relevant topics. Gergen's argument was that cognition, whatever it may be, is inextricably linked with language and thus with communication. This linkage emphasizes the social context of individual cognition and serves to strengthen the concept that individuals can only be understood as part of a social system.

Staddon (1993a) argued that human behavior may be considerably less complex than we would like to think. He argued that psychologists (together with most other people) enjoy the notion that human beings are very complicated, but he also pointed out that there is little empirical evidence to support this notion, a view that was not held by many influential people in the history of psychology.

The major alternatives, as I argue later, lead to a view of human beings that psychologists, in common with the majority of their society, find unpalatable. And it is the unpalatability of more scientifically justifiable alternatives, not the quality or quantity of research evidence for or against the various models, that has led to the development of baroque cognitive models of human behavior.

NEGLECT OF CULTURAL CONTEXT

As I have already pointed out, cognitive and social psychology focus largely on internal processes and tend to downplay or ignore actual behavior (Argyle, 1991). They are based on the implicit assumption that cognitive events are more important, more central to understanding and changing behavior, than are underlying social circumstances (Sampson, 1988). One of the implications of these assumptions is that cultural context, together with social conditions, is marginalized (Jahoda, 1988).

It is clearly neither possible nor desirable to create a science that attempts to explain human behavior while remaining completely divorced from its sociocultural context (Sampson, 1994; Sarason, 1981), but some (e.g., Prilleltensky, 1989) have argued that this is precisely what psychology sets out to do. Our textbooks encourage this view by presenting research in a way that gives the impression that psychology is carried out in a cultural vacuum; the impression is frequently given that "the particular historical period or sociocultural context in which data have been collected is ... of little or no importance" (Spence, 1985, p. 1285). Thus, our training does not promote an awareness of our own cultural assumptions, the cultural assumptions on which research conducted in other countries may be based, or more broadly the differences between political and scientific judgment. As Bailey and Eastman (1994) pointed out, "despite the pretensions of modern psychology, no inquiry is devoid of valuational influence ... [and] .... Even in cognitive psychology, ... the ideology of American individualism shapes questions, forms methods and couches interpretations " (p. 518).

The lack of contextual awareness apparent in mainstream psychology has led to a tendency to treat current local cultural and political climates as if they were absolute (Jahoda, 1988). This in turn can lead to the acceptance of particular cultural or political views as if they reflected a permanent, indisputable reality. Even within cross-cultural psychology, it is frequently assumed that a mere shifting of surface detail will suffice for a mainstream theory to apply in a non-Western culture (Jahoda, 1988). Although there are strong challenges to the assumption that other cultures' ideas are most appropriately interpreted from a Western perspective, this view is not one that fits easily with the approach of mainstream psychology to its subject matter. It is possible that a less culture-bound perspective on human action might produce more flexible and useful models of human action.

Markus and Kitayama (1991), and more recently Rogoff and Chavajay (1995), argued that many of the apparent absolutes in cognitive and social psychology are in fact culture specific. Aspects of the perception of self and others, such as the fundamental attribution error, which have been described by social psychologists as universal characteristics of the thought processes of human adults, may actually be a purely local and temporally specific phenomenon, the result of a particular cultural emphasis on the individual and on competition.

Markus and Kitayama (1991) distinguished between societies in which the self is seen as interdependent and those in which independence is emphasized. People with a culturally acquired interdependent view of the self are likely to make situational attributions for behavior and to describe people in concrete and specific terms, in contrast to members of more individualistic societies who tend to see events as caused dispositionally and to think naturally in terms of general personality traits.

Spence (1985) made a similar point, using research on achievement motivation to illustrate the point that cultural differences in perceptions, both of what achievement is and of how important it is, have been ignored in this field. The dominance of North American researchers in this area, according to Spence (1985), led to an implicit acceptance that characteristics valued in North American society, such as individualism and competition, were universally valuable. In other societies, provision of support to other members of a work group or family has a value equal to or higher than that of individual achievement. However, these instances have either been ignored or regarded as intriguing but essentially anomalous exceptions to a universal rule.

Acceptance of a particular social structure as ahistorical fact can restrict one's view of sociopolitical issues and lead to a narrow and conformist view of society, the individual, and the possible relations between them. Howard

(1985) argued that an awareness of nonepistemic values and of social influences on scientific choices is essential because "current beliefs and assumptions appear to be important determinants of what issues we will choose to study, what findings we expect to obtain, what results we actually obtain, and how we interpret the meaning of those findings" (p. 261). Bailey and Eastman (1994), on a related issue, pointed out that social and behavioral science can only be conducted within some social, moral, and ideological context and that it is important that the specific context and the ways in which it influences all aspects of research should become more explicit within psychology.

PREFERENCE FOR ONE THEORY OVER ANOTHER

Freimuth (1992), considering the grounds that we use to choose one theory over another, argued that scientists, including psychologists, frequently ignore formal epistemic criteria. He argued that theories may be viewed as narratives, constructed stories about the way the world is. From this perspective, a sense of feeling right or of fitting in with an overall view of the world may be more important in selection of a model than is adherence to formal, logical criteria of scientific value.

The role of extrascientific factors in deciding what to study and in what way is by no means unique to psychology. However, implicit political and cultural assumptions have an impact on psychology more directly and more importantly than they do on other fields of scientific endeavor because our subject matter is human beings, who themselves exist in political and cultural contexts.

PREFERENCE FOR COGNITIVE THEORIES

The view that extrascientific values have influenced the development of psychology can hardly be regarded as contentious. As Prilleltensky (1989, p. 795) pointed out, "psychology and society are involved in a network of mutual influences"; the direct influence of broader society has existed since psychology's earliest development and has had a formative effect on the discipline. As I have already argued, judgments based on extrascientific values are by no means unique to psychology, but they are perhaps most dangerously ignored in a field that has human beings as its subject matter.

Examples of the interconnection between sociopolitical movements and academic psychology are easy to find. One example is the history of intelligence testing, an idea initially conceived for the purpose of weeding the feeble-minded out of the French education system, subsequently developed for military selection, and later applied in the eugenics movement (McGaw, 1992). The history of testing suggests that psychology has always been used to serve a variety of social and political ends.

Despite this, psychology has been notably slow to recognize the social influences that have shaped it (Buss, 1975). Scarr (1985), discussing the social context of psychological facts, pointed out that ours is a field in which value judgments are often not identified as such. For example, the concept of psychological androgyny was an invention, not a discovery—an idea that became useful at a particular time because of existing sociopolitical trends (Scarr, 1985). The social and political construction of this concept became obvious to the principal researchers in the field, who wrote about this aspect of the concept extensively (e.g., Bem, 1981), but it received little attention within psychology more generally.

Bem (1974), in the paper that proposed the concept, initially characterized androgyny as a prerequisite for psychological health as if this were an absolute scientific truth, rather than a contention specific to a particular political and social context. A problem with unacknowledged political influence in scientific work is that of how to react when political agendas change, but Bem (1981) addressed this issue head on.

She still wrote positively of " ... the androgynous individual ... who is flexibly masculine or feminine as circumstances warrant " (Bem, 1981, p. 362) and argued that "Politically ... androgyny was a concept ... that appeared to provide a liberated and more humane alternative to the traditional, sex-biased standards of mental health" (p. 362). By 1981, however, she had observed that the concept had had unforeseen and undesired political consequences, and she became one of the few psychologists willing to comment publicly on the relation between the scientific and the political in her own work: " ... the concept of androgyny can also be seen as replacing a prescription to be masculine *or* feminine with the ... prescription to be masculine *and* feminine. The individual now has not one but two potential sources of inadequacy to deal with" (Bem, 1981, p. 363). In a clearly and intentionally political article she wrote that " ... androgyny is insufficiently radical from a feminist perspective" (p. 363).

To reject the concept of androgyny on these grounds, as Bem made clear, is not science. It is politics. Of course, politics cannot and should not be removed from psychological discourse, nor is it possible for gender roles to be studied outside their social context. However, political analysis, when it appears in psychological literature, is frequently not identified as such in the explicit manner adopted by Bem (1981).

Frequently, a confusion occurs within psychology between the task of understanding the world and that of prescribing what sort of a world it should be. To say that "human behaviors and personality attributes should cease to have gender, and society should stop projecting gender into situations irrelevant to genitalia " (Bem, 1981, p. 363) is a perfectly legitimate political statement, but it is not a statement of fact. The point here is not that Bem was deliberately trying to confuse political and scientific thought—she clearly and explicitly was distinguishing between the two—but rather that the general field of psychology is unaccustomed to making this distinction (Prilleltensky, 1992). Thus, psychologists find it extremely difficult to separate the two in a way that is readily acceptable to our peers.

The point of this discussion of androgyny is that a tendency within the discipline to treat the present local cultural and political climate as if it were absolute, a given about human nature, can lead to the promotion of particular views as if they were reflections of permanent, indisputable reality (Spence, 1985). In the case of psychological androgyny, it is possible to appeal to a higher moral authority, arguing that prescription of gender-linked behavior patterns reduces freedom of choice and that the encouragement of individual diversity is morally superior. Such a judgment is culturally, not scientifically, based and, whatever one's personal sympathies, it is important to recognize it as such. Without this recognition, social biases tend to be self-perpetuating, because "the effectiveness of the theory-spawned intervention will be judged in the same cultural context that generated the theories in the first place " (Scarr, 1985, p. 511).

This is a general tendency in psychology, but one that may be particularly important and particularly a matter for concern in applied fields, which deal with issues of social and cultural relevance but lack a tradition of dissension from the status quo (Prilleltensky, 1992). In the next section, I examine some of the extrascientific factors that may have influenced our choice of scientific theories.

Philosophical and Religious Traditions Favor Dualism

Baer, Wolf, and Risley (1987) suggested that we have a culturally acquired tendency to prefer mentalistic explanations of our own behavior. The Cartesian concept of a division of the universe into two fundamentally different kinds of stuff—mind and matter—may seem philosophically naive and old-fashioned, but it remains ingrained in our ways of thinking about the world. Cognitive theories, based on the computer metaphor

(Salzinger, 1992), are clearly dualist in nature (Hineline, 1992; Staddon, 1993a). "To treat the mind as an abstract set of instructions that controls the body is simply to reformulate the traditional dualism of mind and body " (Costall, 1991, p. 157). The computer metaphor has been most clearly rejected by Bevan and Kessel (1994), who pointed out that "metaphors—indeed language in general—can obscure and destroy as well as convey and illuminate " (p. 506). Staddon (1993a) made a similar point in discussing the dualist computer metaphor: "No information is being processed, because nothing is being 'represented ': the external world is changing, neurons are firing, chemicals are circulating and physical actions are occurring" (p. 87).

Massey (1993) argued that one of the most subtly attractive, and most subtly detrimental, aspects of Cartesian dualism is the concept that people are fundamentally different from other animals and operate on entirely different principles. This idea can be traced throughout psychology, from its very earliest beginnings: "He [Fechner] believed in a mental realm with concepts and concepts that owe nothing to biology. Many contemporary cognitive psychologists agree with him" (Staddon, 1993a, p. 9).

Massey (1993) argued that, in the absence of any hard evidence for the contention that humans behave in ways that are fundamentally different from other animals and that have nothing to do with the general principles of biology, modern psychologists should reject any model of human activity that does not apply evenhandedly to animals. Of course, psychologists have not in general followed this advice (Wasserman, 1993), and I contend that this is, at least in part, because it is satisfying to think of human beings as something different from other animals.

Philosophical and Religious Traditions Do Not Favor Behavioral and Socially Determined Views of the Self

Our traditions favor a view of the person not only as a discrete individual, but also as a individual whose essence is a collection of subjective experiences, with a body more or less tacked on as a way of getting around. Our traditions also positively reject alternative views. Hickey (1994), for example, argued that a pervasive social hostility to behaviorism has arisen because behaviorism runs counter to a philosophy that human action is determined by the soul, spirit, or mind, so that the mechanism of human agency lies outside the natural world.

Hineline (1992), arguing along similar lines, hypothesized that mainstream psychologists disliked Skinner's approach to psychology because it challenged the pervasive impression that individuals have control and free will (i.e., the fundamental attribution error, discussed earlier in relation to the cultural relativity of psychological truth. This is an error from which everybody in Western society, even social psychologists, seems to suffer, but that seems to be culturally determined; Markus & Kitayama, 1991). Hineline argued further that Skinner's model of the human organism as one largely controlled by the environment challenged deeply held, culturally determined assumptions about the relation between the person and the world. The idea of the individual as agent, acting on a passive world, is a powerful one in Western society, and one that undermines our ability to consider behavioral concepts objectively.

The only area, according to a discussion by Lamal (1989), in which behaviorism has been permitted to flourish, and an area in which it has had a major impact on quality of human life, has been in the treatment of the developmentally delayed. Lamal (1989) argued that the fact that behaviorism has been generally viewed as an acceptable approach to the developmentally delayed, while it is rejected as an appropriate model for the behavior of "normal " people, suggested a fundamental difference between the way our society views most people and the way in which it views the developmentally delayed. The developmentally delayed, it would appear, are seen as distinctly different from other people. Such a perspective can be seen as comforting, in that it reinforces our own normality by denying the continuum between normal and disordered behavior (Hickey, 1994). Behaviorism is for "animals, the mentally ill, children, and people in institutions " (Locke, 1995, p. 270), but not for us.

The application of behaviorism to solving the problems of normal people is rejected, according to Lamal (1989), because it fails to match our value systems. Simultaneously, scientifically discredited activities such as psychoanalysis and hermeneutics are accorded greater social and cultural respect because they are consistent with a view of the normal, healthy human being as fundamentally a mystic cloud of thought that happens to be attached, inconveniently, to a physical body.

Behavioral principles are acceptable with other animals, with small children, and with the developmentally delayed, but not with normal, fully functioning adults. Somehow we have come to accept an implicit view that we are different from all other organisms. The acceptability of behavioral interventions for developmentally delayed individuals but not for others, in a society that separates mind and body and makes a sharp distinction between people and other animals, also seems to suggest that developmentally delayed humans are implicitly regarded, both by psychologists and more broadly by society as a whole, as a group of people who are essentially damaged or incomplete, susceptible to technological fixes, and thus by definition inferior (Kipnis, 1994). This group may implicitly be seen as less like normal human beings than like other animals. This illiberal view of a particular group of people seems an inevitable consequence of the dominant dualist view of human beings and the sense that thought content defines someone as fully human.

The attractive, culturally reinforced view of the human adult as a fascinating fog of subjective phenomena, loosely attached to a somewhat irrelevant body, stands in stark contrast to the views of early behaviorists. Watson, for example, had a biologist's "faith in the essential simplicity of all behavior ... [and] ... believed human behavior, despite its apparent complexity, to be basically unmysterious and comprehensible" (Staddon, 1993a, pp. 13–14). This is not, however, to imply that behavioral psychology is somehow immune from the political and cultural forces that restrict other aspects of psychology. Although behavioral psychology is founded on a radically different view of the human being, of behavior, of thought, and of the relations between persons and environments, the fact that psychologists are simply not accustomed to thinking in social and political terms affects this area of psychology as well (Prilleltensky, 1992).

Holland (1978) put the view that behaviorists tend to share the individualistic tendencies of other psychologists, examining individual behaviors in individual situations and avoiding major social issues. Although behaviorism has the methods required for an analysis of the structures, systems, and forms of social control that produce individual problems, Holland (1978) argued that behaviorists had avoided these issues and made a call for a stronger emphasis on context in behavioral research.

It seems, however, that the social and professional contingencies that maintain a focus on the individual are not to be lightly cast aside; a decade later, behaviorists such as Malagodi (1986), Burchard (1987), and Prilleltensky (1992) were making much the same arguments and still presenting them as a radical, new, and different departure from the previous literature. Proposals that behavior analysts should expand their domain of interest to include social and political contingencies that shape behavior in the broadest social context, rather than focusing on the narrowly personal, the individual context, and the promotion of strategies to fit people to institutions rather than the other way around, appear regularly in behavioral journals, but their effects on behaviorists' behaviors seem to be negligible.

Braginsky (1985), in a critical analysis of learning-based interventions, argued from the perspective of a nonbehaviorist that behaviorism has suffered from the same self-imposed restrictions as the rest of psychology. She argued that interventions such as token reinforcement programs in prisons and mental hospitals, despite their stated aim of increasing quality of life and promoting rehabilitation, are in fact inevitably repressive and totalitarian. Her point was that the aim of such programs was to introduce competitive capitalism (implicitly assumed to be a normal and desirable state of affairs) to individuals who, for various reasons, deserved the unconditional support of a socialist welfare system.

Prilleltensky (1994a) pointed to a tension in Skinner's writings between descriptions of the potential of behaviorism to advance human welfare and the argument that "good " should be defined in relativistic terms as whatever a specific society chose to reinforce, so that the rhetoric was one of liberalism but the consequences tended to be those of social conservatism. Prilleltensky (1994a) concluded that neither political philosophy was innate in behaviorism, and that behaviorism—as distinct from the social and political views of Skinner—had the potential to foster beneficial social change.

Thus, one may disagree with Braginsky's (1985) contention that behaviorism is necessarily capitalist, individualist, and alienating in ideology, but it is clear that behaviorism often serves to maintain the status quo by regulating and controlling the very people that it claims to be liberating. Behaviorists, in common with cognitive psychologists, have not in general made explicit the possible or probable ideological ramifications of their seemingly nonideological science, and until these ramifications are made explicit and discussed, the potential for the use of behaviorism for the maintenance of undesirable social institutions remains.

PREFERENCE FOR THE COGNITIVE AND INDIVIDUALISTIC IN EXPLANATIONS OF HUMAN BEHAVIOR: POLITICAL AND SOCIOCULTURAL IMPLICATIONS

A professional and scientific culture that places more importance on cognitive events than on objective reality is, as has already been discussed, likely to encourage psychologists to focus interventions on changing cognition rather than altering objective circumstances. Such a tendency will lead to the protection of the status quo and the virtual ignoring of broader cultural and political influences on behavior.

Braginsky (1985) argued that mainstream experimental psychology was "handmaiden of the status quo and of society's prevailing values " (p. 880). By ignoring culture and politics, psychologists, according to Braginsky, have failed to recognize the ideological assumptions underlying their work. She argued that "because mainstream psychology is embedded in the dominant political, economic, and religious ideologies, psychologists have upheld these ideologies rather than examining their impact on the lives of others" (p. 881).

A social and applied psychology that restricts itself to an examination of cognitions thus serves, whether intentionally or not, to divert attention from broader social and political influences on human distress. The role of the psychologist, whether clinical, organisational, educational, or experimental, becomes one of helping individuals to adjust to the existing social order, rather than empowering them to make changes to their environment. Individualism and cognitivism work together to reduce the probability that genuine social inequities will actually be addressed (Prilleltensky, 1990b).

Prilleltensky (1990b), discussing the social and political implications of cognitive psychology, wrote that "the primacy ascribed to the mind and the individual agent in cognitive psychology, in the best Cartesian tradition, tends to reinforce the need to adjust intrapsychic, as opposed to societal, structures in the remediation of personal and social problems" (p. 127). An implicit acceptance of dualism leads to the proposition of an abstract person who exists independent of any sociohistorical context and has cognitions that also exist independent of context. Thus, according to Prilleltensky, the aim of psychological therapy becomes adaptation to the status quo, and the attainment of "a quiet, peaceful and 'rational' acceptance and resignation" (Prilleltensky, 1990b, p. 134) is the final goal. Because its entire focus is on hypothetical events occurring inside individuals' heads, modern clinical psychology is unable to consider the possibility that individual thinking is culturally based (Sampson, 1988) and thus is unable to seek solutions to individual problems in the broader sociocultural context.

The pervasive idea that upsetting events result from maladaptive, dysfunctional thoughts (e.g., Beck, 1984; Meichenbaum, 1974) leads naturally to the idea that the appropriate way to solve personal problems is to focus on changing habitual patterns of thought. This, in turn, leads seemingly inevitably to the conclusion that people are individually responsible for their own problems. Thus, emotional problems are perceived as the result of a failure of the individual to discipline his or her thoughts appropriately; the victims of social inequity or environmental deprivation are, it seems, to blame for their condition (Crawford, 1977).

Psychologists encourage people to manipulate the insides of their heads in order to achieve individual satisfaction rather than to make practical efforts to change the reality that shapes their behavior (Sampson, 1981). In this way, clinical and counseling psychology serves, whether intentionally or not, to divert attention from environmental constraints on behavior and from broader issues of social inequality, poverty, and violence.

This argument has been extended beyond traditionally clinical applications to broader areas of applied psychology. Prilleltensky (1990d), for example, argued that organizational psychologists tended to assume that their services are unambiguously positive and politically noncontentious, acting to enhance both working conditions and worker productivity. However, he argued, organizational psychology is another area in which psychology is applied to the maintenance of the status quo.

Seemingly benign aspects of organizational psychology, such as employee assistance programs, serve to reinforce the concept that employees' problems are internal and subjective and that it is the employee, not the structure of the workplace, that needs to be adjusted. Furthermore, Prilleltensky (1990d) argued, organizational psychology views conflict as interpersonal and thus fails to acknowledge the element of class conflict, of the inevitable conflict of interest between employee and employer. By trying to depoliticize decisions that are fundamentally political, organizational psychology inevitably takes the side of the employer, of the system, and of the status quo. Again, if there is a problem, it is the fault of an individual who does not fit, not of a system that does not provide an appropriate environment.

BROADENING THE FOCUS
OF CONTEMPORARY PSYCHOLOGY

My argument is not that social and cognitive psychologists are part of a deliberate conspiracy to maintain social inequalities. My point is that psychology is often unaware of, and uninterested in, the cultural basis and the cultural implications of its chosen focus. The political and social conservatism that psychology demonstrates is an unintended consequence of the preference for cognitive explanations over their alternatives. The preference itself is a cultural one, and alternative viewpoints, such as the concept that people are primarily physical, chemical, and biological systems, may have quite radical consequences.

Prilleltensky (1990c), for example, has identified four levels of approach to individual psychological problems: the individual, asocial level; the family, milieu, or microsocial level; the community or macrosocial level; and finally a macro-sociopolitical level of analysis and intervention, which would promote consciousness raising, greater dialog between the comfortable academic policymakers and the subjects of those policies, and fundamental societal change. His argument is that psychology has focused its resources on the first and to a lesser degree the second and third while ignoring the fourth. Intervention can be useful at each level, but psychology has not addressed the potential for operating at the broader social levels, where there is much that could be contributed.

Sampson (1988) argued that we need a less mentalistic and more ecologically relevant psychology with a radically new relation to society. It is, of course, possible to disagree, but the point of this chapter is that psychology has traditionally refused to consider this issue. It seems important to develop an awareness of the assumptions that underlie modern psychology. We need to become aware of the vested interests we are supporting and then to consider whether we are acting in the most effective way in order to achieve the goal of understanding human behavior in context.

Chapter 9

New Directions: Alternatives
to a Monolithic Psychology of Cognition

A string of raw facts; a little gossip and wrangle about opinions; a little classification and description on the mere descriptive level; a strong prejudice that we have states of mind, but not a single law in the sense that physics shows us laws, not a single proposition from which any consequence causally can be deduced. We don't even know the terms between which the elementary laws would obtain if we had them.

—James (1893, p. 468)

If cognitivism is scientifically invalid and based on outdated and inappropriate metaphysical concepts, what does this imply for the development of the discipline? Does it mean that psychology has met a dead end?

Proponents of cognitivism, through their identification of psychology with the study of cognitions, have placed unnecessary limits on the development of the field. The unwillingness to consider alternative approaches, the approach by which "cognitivism admits of no alternative, since any alternative must be something other than psychology " (Bolton, 1991, p. 104) means that challenges to a single, monolithic, cognitive study of psychology have, for the mainstream, simply been defined out of existence. Psychology is cognitivism, and cognitivism is psychology. Costall (1991) argued that the underlying computer metaphor, the dualist basis for so much cognitive theorizing, has become so widespread among psychologists that we have lost awareness that it is a metaphor, and psychologists are increasingly accepting the literal view that brains are computers.

Conformity of thought and rejection of alternative viewpoints tend to lead to an artificial narrowing of perspective on the subject matter. Thus, when cognitivism is eventually acknowledged to be theoretically barren, psychology as a whole would appear to be left with nowhere to go.

Of course, "cognitivism represents an unprecedented unity of purpose within academic psychology " (Costall, 1991, p. 152). Psychology has a history of fragmentation, combined with frequent claims that this fragmentation is evidence that psychology is inferior to other, more unified fields of endeavor. Psychologists are frequently criticized for our pre-paradigmatic and disorganized state, and we are urged to work for the development of a grand unified theory (e.g., Staats, 1989, 1991).

It is clear that the concept of a grand unified theory of psychology, similar to the paradigms that unify physics or chemistry, is deeply satisfying. However, unity per se has no intrinsic value. It is the adequacy of the united approach that is important. In this chapter, I argue that the identification of cognitivism as our grand unified theory (e.g., Sperry, 1993) produces a false and premature unity and that psychology needs to explore as many other alternative explanatory models as possible.

Clearly, the notion that thought is relatively unimportant in human action is an unpopular one, but unpopularity does not make it wrong. Of course, it appears obvious that we act the way we do because we think the way we do, but it is important to remember that our own personal, implicit models of how human beings work are based on commonsense perspectives that are internally contradictory and frequently wrong (Kelley, 1992). Many psychologists seem unaware of the nonempirical basis of their most fundamental beliefs about human beings. As scientists we need to accept that everything is open to question and that the most fundamentally obvious facts that underpin a theory may well turn out to be the ones that are wrong (Chalmers, 1982).

It may be most appropriate to look for a solution to these problems in models that unseat cognition from its central role in human action. Psychology's trend toward unification has been premature because the unifying paradigm of cognitivism has nothing to offer beyond its power to unify. It does not provide an adequate explanation of behavior, or even a more adequate explanation than previous and alternative theories.

A period of diversity may be essential in the search for models that are able to explain human behavior in all its complexity, not by invocation of a ghost in the machine but by taking a scientific and unsuperstitious approach to the subject matter. Diversity is no more valuable for its own sake than is unity, but it may be desirable if it may eventually lead to a different and more adequate unifying model.

ECLECTICISM:
ONLY AN APPARENT SOLUTION

I am not advocating a style of eclectic psychology in which all theories are equally right, in which "all have won and all should have prizes " (Luborsky, Singer, & Luborsky, 1975). It is important to distinguish eclecticism, the use of any theory or model that seems to work best to solve a specific problem at a specific time, from a relativistic approach to psychology that encourages diversity of theoretical development but insists that each theory identify its own boundaries and justify itself in its own terms (Greenwald, Pratkanis, Leippe, & Baumgardner, 1986).

Eclectic therapy is frequently justified on the grounds that it maximizes gains for the client, at least in the immediate term. From the point of view of a clinician seeking to relieve a client's distress, it seems more practical and more ethically appropriate to provide some sort of treatment or intervention, even if it is less than ideally optimal, than it is to wait until a clearer theoretical overview of the topic emerges.

Promotion of an eclectic approach to psychological theory may also seem a relatively trouble-free position to hold, although the person who benefits in this case is not the client but the psychologist. Eclecticism in research and theory seems readily acceptable to us as individuals because it seems to fit with a liberal–democratic view of individual intellectual freedoms within a community of scholars, as well as with the broader notion of the human right to freedom of thought and expression. As a unifying approach to psychology, it is also acceptable for another reason: It does not demand any change in our own behavior. An eclectic approach to theory positively rejects the consideration of the relative merits of alternative approaches; the call is merely for tolerance. Academics can declare their agreement with eclecticism and diversity in principle, support other people's right to do whatever they like in the name of psychological research, and simultaneously affirm their own right to ignore alternative approaches and go on with what they have been doing all along.

Theoretical eclecticism does not lack for critics. Nor is it possible to divorce an eclectic approach to practical intervention, justified in terms of benefit to clients, from the theoretical understanding of human action. Hallam (1987) pointed out that eclecticism as a strategy, whether in therapy or in research, maximizes short-term gains at the expense of long-term development. In a similar vein, Wolpe (1989) argued that eclectic approaches to therapy must inevitably weaken theoretical and research development. The adoption of approaches that lack a scientific basis, he argued, would lead to research that evaluated existing strategies and would thus prevent the coherent development of well-understood models, from which it might be possible to gain a clearer theoretical understanding of human behavior and, as a consequence, develop different and more effective strategies for behavior change.

The drift within therapy toward "boxes of tricks " and an emphasis on techniques rather than understanding has been criticized by other writers (e.g., Branch, 1987; Hayes, Rincover, & Solnick, 1980). A theory-based approach to therapy permits the scientific development of techniques, together with an understanding of how they may operate and what their limits may be, whereas eclecticism "resembles having one's feet firmly planted in midair " (Branch, 1987, p. 79). If using a single inadequate theory causes problems, then mixing several inadequate theories, without making explicit which ones might be used in which circumstances and why, merely compounds the problem. Thus, eclecticism in the absence of a critical comparison of different theories in different situations, in the absence of any attempt to refine different approaches or to define their boundaries, is theoretically sterile and cannot lead to the development of a unified and scientific psychology.

MINI PARADIGMS:
COGNITIVISM IN CONTEXT

Although cognitive models are inadequate to deal with the entire subject matter of psychology, it is clear that they are not completely without value. The theories cannot be ignored, and they should not be rejected out of hand. Yet we need a clearer awareness of their limitations; cognitive theories do not explain every aspect of human behavior. As I suggested in chapter 3, a more scientific and clearly delimited cognitive psychology, one that does not seek to monopolize psychology but aims somewhat more modestly to explain some human actions in some circumstances, would be more valuable.

In place of the proposition that cognition is the only relevant cause of everything that a psychologist may legitimately study, one might propose that conscious thoughts are the proximal determinants of actions under some circumstances but not others, or that conscious thoughts are the proximal determinants of some classes of behavior but not others, or (combining these two) that conscious thoughts determine only some classes of behavior in only some classes of situation.

Starting with a partial model such as this for the relation between some cognitions and some behaviors in some contexts, the question of defining limits becomes immediately apparent. By defining limits, one may be able to specify situations in which certain cognitions may be relevant and thus develop a theory that is both more testable and more useful. Greenwald et al. (1986) proposed a general approach to psychological research, that of searching for the limits and conditions under which particular hypotheses hold, which may facilitate research progress. They argued that exploration of the limits of applicability of specific theories can tell us a great deal about the adequacy of our theories and about the conditions that appear to influence the validity of those theories.

DEVELOPING NONCOGNITIVE ALTERNATIVES

The cognitive bias in modern psychology has obscured continuing advances in behavioral theory (Eifert & Plaud, 1993; Plaud & Vogeltanz, 1993). Behavioral models exist that explain a range of human behaviors generally regarded as obviously cognitive in nature, from specific instances such as Eisenberger's (1992) learned industriousness concept, which provides a learning theory explanation for the work ethic, to general and far-reaching models that explain essential human characteristics such as language in behavioral terms (Hayes & Hayes, 1992).

Learning theory has been rejected prematurely by the mainstream, and its full implications have yet to be developed (Biglan, 1993). Acierno, Hersen, Van Hasselt, and Ammerman (1994) argued that both cognitivism and the adoption of an eclectic approach are based on the presumed limitations of behavioral methods. However, they argued, we have yet to establish the conditions under which specific behavioral principles and strategies are or are not effective. Although "the limitations of early conditioning models and treatments have led many behavior therapists to abandon conditioning principles and replace them with loosely defined cognitive theories and treatments" (Eifert, Forsyth, & Schauss, 1993, p. 107), the cognitive models replacing them are not an improvement. Eifert and Plaud (1993), in a critical analysis of cognitive alternatives to behavioral psychology, asked, "where ... have the conceptual foundations of the various cognitive–behavioral theories and treatments been adequately defined and elaborated on? " (p. 103) and warned that "increased preoccupation with hypothesized inner processes will weaken the behavior therapy movement unless theories about private events are appropriately related to and integrated with basic behavioral concepts and research findings" (p. 103). Modern developments in behavioral theory may provide more fertile ground for development than the sterile metaphors of the cognitivists (Eifert et al., 1993).

On similar lines, Salzinger (1992) argued that cognitive techniques have added nothing to our understanding of behavior or our ability to treat psychological distress; they simply cloak legitimate behavioral techniques in language that obfuscates rather than illuminates the underlying processes. He urged therapists to pay attention to continuing developments in behavior theory and therapy, in particular to the growing understanding of the need to assess reinforcement history, and to the increasing attention paid to discriminative stimuli. Explicit and systematic attention to these variables, he argued, is more likely to produce theoretical and therapeutic advances than is a concentration on self-reports independent of the setting events that may elicit them.

The next section of this chapter explores the contextualist behaviorist approach, a development that aims to combine a noncognitive approach to human behavior with an increased emphasis on the influences of the physical, social, and cultural context on that behavior (e.g., Biglan, 1993). Thus, the interactions between contextual cues and individual behaviors, rather than behaviors themselves, become the focus of analysis.

Contextualism is not purely a behavioral movement. The area of social psychophysiology, for example, is based on the premise that physiological events can only be fully understood within their specific social and physical context (Cacioppo & Berntson, 1992; Cacioppo, Berntson & Andersen, 1991). A more generally contextualist approach to human behavior, independent of the behavioral approach (Jaeger & Rosnow, 1988), holds that all conceptions of human action must take an active, dynamic, and developmental context into account. Although this is not a behavioral analysis, it starts from the same assumptions that context is not a setting event but an integral part of any act. Despite these other strands of argument, it is within the behavioral paradigm that contextualism is currently receiving the most attention.

Contextualist Behaviorism

Contextualist behaviorism is not a radical departure in the thinking of behaviorists (Morris, 1988). Rather, it is an organic change, a broadening of perspective that has arisen at least in part as a response to a frustration with an individual-focused psychology despite problems with clear social and cultural contexts (Biglan, 1993).

Traditionally the focus in behaviorism has been on the organism, the behavior, and its consequences. Contextualist behaviorism maintains this approach but increases the focus on the role of environmental stimuli in evoking behavior. In one sense, contextualist behaviorism may be considered to be little more than a rediscovery of the discriminative stimulus. In another sense, it provides new avenues for a behavioral approach to understanding human actions within social, physical, and personal contexts (Morris, 1988).

Biglan, Glasgow, and Singer (1990) argued that a behavioral contextualist analysis, which enables individuals to be viewed in a wider context without relinquishing the principles of objectivity and a focus on the observable, may be necessary in order to progress with our understanding of many behavioral problems. Dumas (1989), for example, discussed the behavioral assessment of children from a contextualist perspective. He argued that the traditional focus on the individual's behavior, rather than on the events that elicit that behavior, leads to an assumption that the context is static and unchangeable. However, physical, social, and cultural conditions are dynamic and continuously changing, and thus context may have profound effects on the relations between behaviors and their outcomes. A consideration of context may also help the behaviorist to identify classes of behaviors that may have functional equivalence or at least may be part of a more complex class of responses perhaps overlooked by a more individual-centered analysis. Contextualist behavior analysis is not about behaviors but about the functions or purposes of those behaviors (Carr, 1993). Behaviors are not identical to their individual components. Rather, they should be understood in context, as instances of response classes (Delprato, 1993) or as actions (Lee, 1993).

An individual-centered approach leads to an assumption that the broader context within which behaviors occur is off limits for the psychologist (Prilleltensky, 1990b). By contrast, a contextualist approach views the individual-in-context as the unit of analysis (Morris, 1988).

Biglan et al. (1990) pointed out that an individual-centered approach to problems is often unable to produce results because it is unable to identify, let alone address, systemic inequities such as poverty and the resulting lack of resources to support individual behavior change. Contextualism may be useful in the development of principles that deal with social units. In approaching such problems from the standpoint of contextualist behaviorism, Biglan et al. (1990) emphasized the importance of identifying manipulable variables. The approach focuses on the identification and modification of contexts that promote problem behaviors in individuals with particular learning histories and not simply on the description of those contexts. For example, they advocated an objective assessment of a person's exposure to aversive life events and exposure, or lack of exposure, to educational and health-enhancing contexts; this assessment provides useful and specific information about a person's reinforcement history and likely future behavior. They contrasted this fine-grained contextualist approach with the traditional tendency among psychologists to record demographic variables such as ethnicity, gender, or social class and then treat them as if they could provide explanations of behavior.

Cultural practices, they argued, could be studied in the same way as individual behaviors. For example, the high rates of teenage pregnancy in certain communities (Hechtman, 1989) might be studied not in terms of individuals' fecklessness, lack of planning, or ignorance, but in terms of the relation between sexual behavior and contextual aspects that reinforce or provide setting events for such behavior. Evidence (e.g., Battle, 1990; Burton, 1990; Geronimus, 1992) suggests that teenage preganacy is contextually supported in some sectors of American society; the assumption that it may be explained in terms of dysfunctional individual behavior is rejected. Cultural practices, whether teenage motherhood or systems of government, will survive only if their outcomes sustain those who carry out the activity.

If cognitive psychology has sought to explain too much with too few concepts and too little awareness of its own limitations, behavioral psychology has traditionally been guilty of the opposite. Behaviorists, with the distinguished exception of Skinner (e.g., 1984, 1985, 1986) have tended to focus exclusively on individual behaviors.

Jason and Glenwick (1984), in a review of behavioral community psychology published over a decade ago, asked, "is it possible that some of our primary preventive interventions are merely teaching youngsters how to fit in better and be less of a nuisance?... how frequently do behavioral psychologists examine whether our policies support societal immobility, sexism, socioeconomic class discrimination, and excessive adult control" (p. 109). The argument that behavioral interventions have focused on training for docility and obedience was raised by Winett and Winkler (1972) even earlier.

Holland (1978) argued that behaviorists must be willing to apply their models to the big social issues; behaviorism, he proposed, should be applied to the analysis of the structures, systems, and forms of social control that produce the context within which individual problem behaviors are elicited. Burchard (1987) made a similar point within the context of the prevention of delinquent behavior, arguing that behaviorists must expand their domain of interest to include the broad social and political contingencies that turn young people toward crime; they should not simply focus on the personal, family, and school context. A behavioral understanding of racism, unemployment, and the gap between the rich and poor might go a long way toward a clearer understanding of how any one particular individual comes to engage in or to avoid criminal activity.

Behavioral contextualism is not without its critics. Marr (1993) acknow-ledged the need for a scientific study on human action in context, which he contrasted positively with the mystical nonmaterialism of cognitive psy-chology: "For many cognitive psychologists,... human behaviors emerge like wraiths out of a mysterious cauldron of processed images, thoughts, strategies, schemas, rules, and representations, all apparently disembodied from history and current contingencies" (Marr, 1993, p. 59). He also stressed that the same mystical lack of clarity could arise within contextu-alism: "Context, improperly treated, can easily become an eerie aura surrounding a functional account, as well as an infinite well of explanatory appeal" (p. 61).

On similar grounds, Shull and Lawrence (1993) argued that a strongly contextualist view, incorporating a reluctance to examine the component parts of specific instances, was of no more use than the scientifically discredited schools of gestalt and transpersonal psychology. Staddon (1993b) also criticized the imprecision of contemporary contextualist analysis, although he acknowledged that imprecision may be inevitable in the early stages of the development of a discipline and that it is not necessarily intrinsic to that discipline in the sense in which imprecision is intrinsic to cognitive models.

The behavioral–contextualist view, that it is possible to combine a rigorously objective and nonmediational approach to human behavior with a perspective that takes the sociopolitical context into account, has clear political implications that must be acknowledged. Such approaches may lead to a radically new approach to understanding human choices and to empowering individuals to attain more positive experiences.

Behavior in Context: A Sociopolitical Psychology of Behavior

An emphasis on the context may have the potential to lead to a radically different type of psychology, a psychology that focuses not only on the individual but with equal force on the social forces that influence individual choices. Such a theoretical focus can potentially lead to radically different practical implications. It is important, however, to keep in mind that such a theoretical focus is inevitably political, and it is important when dealing with these topics that the political biases and attitudes of researchers are made explicit and their impact on scientific analysis acknowledged.

For example, Biglan et al. (1990) argued that interventions to reduce cigarette smoking would be ineffective as long as they assumed that smoking was purely a matter of individual choice and focused exclusively on persuading the individual not to start or not to continue smoking. Biglan et al. (1990) pointed to economic structures that encouraged tobacco companies to promote smoking and to social structures that provided a context in which smoking was not simply acceptable but was in fact a positive symbol of maturity and desirability. From a contextualist point of view, it seems clear that there can be no real reduction in tobacco usage, and thus of preventable deaths from cancer and heart disease, unless interventions are put in place that will change the social, political, and economic environment that currently supports individuals' decisions to smoke and constrains their choice of avoiding cigarettes.

Taking a contextualist approach to tobacco control involves changing one's perspective, away from strategies to help individuals resist pressures to smoke and toward strategies to reduce those pressures. These strategies might include political changes that many might find unacceptable, for example, governments providing incentives for corporations to reduce their financial dependence on the sale of tobacco products; tax and excise disincentives for the promotion and sale of these products; or legislation for physical and social environments in which smoking behavior receives no extrinsic reinforcement (Biglan et al., 1990). Such proposals have powerful political implications that need to be explicitly acknowledged and carefully weighed in the process of developing strategies and policy recommendations. However, concentrating on the individual smoker has political implications as well, and these are rarely acknowledged.

Prilleltensky (1989, 1990a, 1990b, 1990c, 1990d, 1992) has repeatedly taken an explicitly political approach to contextualist psychology. His basic premise has been that psychology's focus on cognition has led to an overemphasis on changing the individual to fit the social context and a relative lack of consideration of the possibility that social contexts may be serving to maintain individual distress. Prilleltensky (1992) stressed that recognizing the locus of problems may lie outside the individual is only the first step in a radical and contextualist psychology. Psychology, according to Prilleltensky, has a moral obligation to work toward the establishment of social conditions conducive to a good society. Psychology has a strong record of considering the moral obligations of individual practitioners and researchers toward individual clients and research participants, but it has traditionally ignored the broader moral imperative to society as a whole.

Prilleltensky (1994b) pointed out that a focus on scientific research can never lead to a definitive statement on the ethics or morals of psychology. We need to start with a moral and ethical viewpoint, not hope it will emerge from our data (Bailey & Eastman, 1994). Data are always political, psychology is already a political and moral force, and the issue is that of recognizing the political implications of psychology as it is practiced and then deciding whether we find them personally, morally, and ethically acceptable.

A difficulty with this approach, of course, is the question of who decides what defines a good society. It has been proposed that objective definitions of good are possible (e.g., Plaud & Vogeltanz, 1994), with reference to community consensus and similar concepts. However, reference to concepts such as that which is reinforcing to the dominant culture are highly problematic (Bailey & Eastman, 1994). Malagodi (1986) made the point that our culture contains many practices, for example our assumption that totally effective waste management is too expensive to be worthwhile, which work against the well-being of its members, and indeed against the culture's chances of survival.

The aim of science, to describe and explain the world, is incompatible with the aim of deciding what that world ought to be (Bailey & Eastman, 1994). Moral decisions are not scientific decisions; they can not arise from an objective consideration of value-free data, because the collection and analysis of psychological data cannot be conducted in a value-free manner (Kendler, 1993). Therefore, it is necessary that psychologists recognize the political assumptions that underlie their work rather than hope that political good will somehow emerge from it (Prilleltensky, 1992, 1994b).

Prilleltensky (1990a), urging a radical politicizing of psychology, argued that modern Western societies are not good societies in either philosophical or pragmatic terms. He proposed psychological intervention techniques for consciousness-raising—deconstructing and demystifying the "ideological messages that distort people's awareness of socio-political circumstances that shape their lives " (p. 311)—and for developing and elaborating means for structural change. He argued that cultural hegemony, the process by which a problem is defined in individualistic or other nonsocial terms, is a powerful force for conservatism. Psychologists who accept culturally defined definitions of distress as individually caused are serving to maintain the status quo. Prilleltensky (1990a) advocated that psychologists should critically examine their clinical practice for individualistic bias, and in their role as teachers and researchers they should encourage doubt, be explicit about the rules of discourse, and examine the limits of individualistic models.

Obviously, these arguments are prompted by a particular view of what constitutes a good society. However, Prilleltensky's argument is that all psychology is based on political beliefs about what is desirable; he is merely more open about his personal political stance than are most psychologists. Political perspective, according to Prilleltensky, is not something to be left politely out of psychological discussions but something that must be addressed in considering the implications of any theoretical stance.

In an article dealing with the prevention of psychopathology, Albee (1986) also pointed to some of the political and social consequences of an individualistic approach. The imperfect analogy between mental illness and physical illness, he argued, has resulted in a tendency to ignore the fact that mental illnesses are not discrete disease entities that some individuals "have" and the rest of us do not. Rather, the majority of diagnosed disorders represent the end of a continuum from normal behavior, a set of responses learned as a result of social circumstances, particularly the effects of stress, powerlessness, and exploitation. (This is not, of course, to deny that some mental illnesses have biochemical or genetic causes but merely to remind us that this is not true in every case.)

Albee (1986) inferred from this argument that social change might have a greater effect in reducing psychopathology than would a focus on treating the individual, a focus arising from an individual-centered view of mental illness. He argued that most psychopathology could be prevented by social change—major adjustments to society, not to isolated individuals, with the aim of eliminating damaging childhood experiences, poverty, powerlessness, low self-esteem, loneliness, and social isolation. Again, the political assumptions underlying this argument are diametrically opposed to those underlying cognitive therapy, but the fact that the political perspective is clearly articulated does not make Albee's views any more political than mainstream views.

Prilleltensky (1990d) conducted a similar analysis of the sociopolitical implications of industrial–organizational psychology. Psychologists, he argued, tend to assume that they are providing an apolitical service equally valuable to employers and employees. However, industrial psychology again tends to maintain the status quo. If employees have work-related problems, the employee and not the work situation needs to change. Organizational psychology personalizes a political conflict between employer and employee and ignores the fundamentally different expectations and goals of the two groups. Fundamental social problems cannot be solved through cognitive psychology. As Morf (1994) put it, phenomenology is not going to save the world.

In conclusion, let me quote Skinner (1977) once more. "We choose the wrong path at the very start when we suppose that our goal is to change the 'minds and hearts of men and women' rather than the world in which we live" (p. 10). There is considerable social hostility to a behaviorist and scientific understanding of human behavior, a hostility that arises from a discomfort with models that run counter to our dominant dualist philosophy, from an uneasiness concerning the implications of such models for potentially radical social change, and from a desire to maintain a comfortable view of psychological distress as something different from ordinary behavior, not a natural consequence of the society in which we live (Hickey, 1994).

We are not qualitatively different from other animals. We, like they, exist solely in the physical, material world. If we have delusions of grandeur that help us to endure this reality, then let us see these for what they are—escape attempts, and not reality.

References

Abramson, L. Y., & Alloy, L. B. (1981). Depression, nondepression, and cognitive illusions: Reply to Schwartz. *Journal of Experimental Psychology: General, 100,* 436–447.

Abramson, L. Y., Seligman, M. E. P., & Teasdale, J. D. (1978). Learned helplessness in humans: Critique and reformulation. *Journal of Abnormal Psychology, 87,* 49–74.

Acierno, R., Hersen, M., Van Hasselt, V. B., & Ammerman, R. T. (1994). Remedying the Achilles heel of behavior research and therapy: Prescriptive matching of intervention and psychopathology. *Journal of Behavior Therapy and Experimental Psychiatry, 25,* 179–188.

Ackermann, R., & DeRubeis, R. J. (1991). Is depressive realism real? *Clinical Psychology Review, 11,* 565–584.

Adelman, P. K., & Zajonc, R. B. (1989). Facial efference and the experience of emotion. *Annual Review of Psychology, 40,* 249–280.

Ajzen, I. (1991). The theory of planned behavior. *Organizational Behavior and Human Decision Processes, 50,* 179–211.

Ajzen, I., & Fishbein, M. (1970). The prediction of behavior from attitudinal and normative variables. *Journal of Experimental Social Psychology, 6,* 466–487.

Ajzen, I., & Fishbein, M. (1980). *Understanding attitudes and predicting social behavior.* Englewood Cliffs, NJ: Prentice-Hall.

Ajzen, I., & Madden, T. J. (1986). Prediction of goal-directed behavior: Attitudes, intentions, and perceived behavioral control. *Journal of Experimental Social Psychology, 22,* 453–474.

Albee, G. W. (1986). Towards a just society: Lessons from observations on the primary prevention of psychopathology. *American Psychologist, 41,* 891–898.

Alloy, L. B., & Abramson, L. Y. (1979). Judgment of contingency in depressed and nondepressed students: Sadder but wiser? *Journal of Experimental Psychology: General, 108,* 441–485.

Alloy, L. B., Abramson, L. Y., & Viscusi, D. (1981). Induced mood and the illusion of control. *Journal of Personality and Social Psychology, 41,* 1129–1140.

Alloy, L. B., & Ahrens, A. H. (1987). Depression and pessimism for the future: Biased use of statistically relevant information in predictions for self versus others. *Journal of Personality and Social Psychology, 52,* 366–378.

Alloy, L. B., & Clements, C. M. (1992). Illusion of control: Invulnerability to negative affect and depressive symptoms after laboratory and natural stressors. *Journal of Abnormal Psychology, 101,* 234–245.

Altmaier, E. M., Russell, D. W., Kao, C. F., Lehmann, T. R., & Weinstein, J. N. (1993). Role of self-efficacy in rehabilitation outcome among chronic low back pain patients. *Journal of Counseling Psychology, 40,* 335–339.

Ambrose, B., & Rholes, W. S. (1993). Automatic cognitions and the symptoms of depression and anxiety in children and adolescents: An examination of the content specificity hypothesis. *Cognitive Therapy and Research, 17,* 289–308.

Argyle, M. (1991). A critique of cognitive approaches to social judgments and social behavior. In J. P. Forgas (Ed.), *Emotion and social judgments* (pp. 161–178). New York: Pergamon.

Awad, A. (1990). Behavior therapy ranked among most cited journals. *Behavior Therapist, 13,* 120.

Baer, D. M., Holt, C. S., & Lichtenstein, E. (1986). Self-efficacy and smoking re-examined: Construct validity and clinical utility. *Journal of Consulting and Clinical Psychology, 54,* 846–852.

Baer, D. M., Wolf, M. M., & Risley, T. R. (1987). Some still-current dimensions of applied behavior analysis. *Journal of Applied Behavior Analysis, 20,* 313–327.

Bagozzi, R. P. (1981). Attitudes, intentions, and behavior: A test of some key hypotheses. *Journal of Personality and Social Psychology, 41,* 607–627.

Bailey, J. R., & Eastman, W. N. (1994). Positivism and the promise of the social sciences. *Theory and Psychology, 4,* 505–524.

Baker, T. B., Cannon, D. S., Tiffany, S. T., & Gino, A. (1984). Cardiac response as an index of the effect of aversion therapy. *Behaviour Research and Therapy, 22,* 403–411.

Bandura, A. (1977). Self-efficacy: Toward a unifying theory of behavior change. *Psychological Review, 84,* 191–215.

Bandura, A. (1978). Reflections on self-efficacy. *Advances in Behaviour Research and Therapy, 1,* 237–269.

Bandura, A. (1980). Gauging the relationship between self-efficacy judgment and action. *Cognitive Therapy and Research, 4,* 263–268.

Bandura, A. (1981). In search of pure unidirectional determinants. *Behavior Therapy, 12,* 30–40.

Bandura, A. (1982). Self-efficacy mechanism in human agency. *American Psychologist, 37,* 122–147.

Bandura, A. (1983). Temporal dynamics and decomposition of reciprocal determinism: A reply to Phillips and Orton. *Psychological Review, 90,* 166–170.

Bandura, A. (1984). Recycling misconceptions of perceived self-efficacy. *Cognitive Therapy and Research, 8,* 231–255.

Bandura, A. (1986). *Social foundations of thought and action.* Englewood Cliffs, NJ: Prentice-Hall.

Bandura, A. (1991). Social cognitive theory of self-regulation. *Organizational Behavior and Human Decision Processes, 50,* 248–287.

Bandura, A., Adams, N. E., & Beyer, J. (1977). Cognitive processes mediating behavioral change. *Journal of Personality and Social Psychology, 35,* 125–139.

Bandura, A., Reese, L., & Adams, N. E. (1982). Microanalysis of action and fear arousal as a function of differential levels of perceived self-efficacy. *Journal of Personality and Social Psychology, 43,* 5–21.

Bandura, A., Taylor, C. B., Williams, S. L., Mefford, I. N., & Barchas, J. D. (1985). Catecholamine secretion as a function of perceived coping efficacy. *Journal of Consulting and Clinical Psychology, 53,* 406–414.

Barnard, M. E., & DiGiuseppe, R. A. (1989). *Inside rational emotive therapy.* New York: Academic Press.

Baron, J. (1988). *Thinking and deciding.* Cambridge, England: Cambridge University Press.

Barrios, B. A. (1983). The role of cognitive mediators in heterosocial anxiety: A test of self-efficacy theory. *Cognitive Therapy and Research, 7,* 543–554.

Battle, S. F. (1990). Changing family roles. *Journal of Health and Social Policy, 1,* 27–38.

Beck, A. T. (1963). Thinking and depression: Idiosyncratic content and cognitive distortions. *Archives of General Psychiatry, 9,* 324–333.

Beck, A. T. (1976). *Cognitive therapy and the emotional disorders.* New York: International Universities Press.

Beck, A. T. (1984). Cognition and therapy. *Archives of General Psychiatry, 41,* 1112–1114.

Beck, A. T. (1991). Cognitive therapy: A 30-year retrospective. *American Psychologist, 46,* 368–375.

Beck, A. T. (1993). Cognitive therapy: Past, present, and future. *Journal of Consulting and Clinical Psychology, 61,* 194–198.

Beck, A. T., Rush, A. J., Shaw, B. F., & Emery, G. (1979). *Cognitive therapy of depression.* New York: Guilford.

Beidel, D. C., & Turner, S. M. (1986). A critique of the theoretical bases of cognitive–behavioral theories and therapy. *Clinical Psychology Review, 6,* 177–197.

Bem, D. J. (1972). Self-perception theory. In L. Berkowitz (Ed.), *Advances in experimental social psychology, Volume 16* (pp. 1–62). New York: Academic Press.

Bem, S. L. (1974). The measurement of psychological androgyny. *Journal of Consulting and Clinical Psychology, 42,* 155–162.

Bem, S. L. (1981). Gender schema theory: A cognitive account of sex typing. *Psychological Review, 88,* 354–364.

Benassi, V. A., & Mahler, H. I. M. (1985). Contingency judgments by depressed college students: Sadder but not always wiser. *Journal of Personality and Social Psychology, 49,* 1323–1329.

Bernier, M., & Avard, J. (1986). Self-efficacy, outcome, and attrition in a weight-reduction program. *Cognitive Therapy and Research, 10,* 319–338.

Bernieri, F. J. (1988). Coordinated movement and rapport in teacher–student interactions. *Journal of Nonverbal Behavior, 12,* 120–138.

Bernieri, F. J., Davis, J. M., Rosenthal, R., & Knee, C. (1991, September). *Interactional synchrony and the social affordance of rapport: A validation study.* Paper presented at the 99th annual conference of the American Psychological Association, San Francisco, CA.

Bernieri, F. J., Reznick, J. S., & Rosenthal, R. (1988). Synchrony, pseudosynchrony, and dissynchrony: Measuring the entrainment process in mother–infant interactions. *Journal of Personality and Social Psychology, 54,* 243–253.

Bernieri, F. J., & Rosenthal, R. (1991). Interpersonal coordination: Behavior matching and interactional synchrony. In R. S. Feldman & B. Rime (Eds.), *Fundamentals of nonverbal behavior* (pp. 401–432). New York: Cambridge University Press.

Betz, N. E., & Hackett, G. (1981). The relationship of career-related self-efficacy expectations to perceived career options in college men and women. *Journal of Counseling Psychology, 28,* 399–410.

Bevan, W., & Kessel, F. (1994). Plain truths and home cooking: Thoughts on the making and remaking of psychology. *American Psychologist, 49,* 505–509.

Biglan, A. (1987). A behavior-analytic critique of Bandura's self-efficacy theory. *Behavior Analyst, 10,* 1–15.

Biglan, A. (1993). Recapturing Skinner's legacy to behavior therapy. *Behavior Therapist, 16,* 3–5.

Biglan, A., Glasgow, R. E., & Singer, G. (1990). The need for a science of larger social units: A contextual approach. *Behavior Therapy, 21,* 195–215.

Biran, M., & Wilson, G. T. (1981). Treatment of phobic disorders using cognitive and exposure methods: A self-efficacy analysis. *Journal of Consulting and Clinical Psychology, 49,* 886–899.

Blaney, P. H. (1986). Affect and memory: A review. *Psychological Bulletin, 99,* 229–246.

Block, J., & Colvin, C. R. (1994). Positive illusions and well-being revisited: Separating fiction from fact. *Psychological Bulletin, 116,* 28.

Bolton, N. (1991). Cognitivism: A phenomenological critique. In A. Still & A. Costall (Eds.), *Against cognitivism: Alternative foundations for cognitive psychology* (pp. 104–121). New York: Harvester Wheatsheaf.

Bootzin, R. R. (1985). Affect and cognition in behavior therapy. In S. Reiss & R. R. Bootzin (Eds.), *Theoretical issues in behavior therapy* (pp. 35–45). New York: Academic Press.

Borkovec, T. D. (1978). Self efficacy: Cause or reflection of behaviour change? *Advances in Behaviour Research and Therapy, 1,* 163–170.

Bornstein, R. F. (1992). Subliminal mere exposure effects. In R. F. Bornstein & T. S. Pittman (Eds.), *Perception without awareness: Cognitive, clinical, and social perspectives* (pp. 191–210). New York: Guilford.

Bornstein, R. F., & Pittman, T. S. (Eds.). (1992). *Perception without awareness: Cognitive, clinical, and social perspectives.* New York: Guilford.

Bower, G. H. (1981). Mood and memory. *American Psychologist, 36,* 129–148.

Bower, G. H. (1991). Mood congruity of social judgments. In J. P. Forgas (Ed.), *Emotion and social judgments* (pp. 31–53). New York: Pergamon.

Bozoian, S., Rejeski, W. J., & McAuley, E. (1994). Self-efficacy influences feeling states associated with acute exercise. *Journal of Sport and Exercise Psychology, 16,* 326–333.

Braginsky, D. D. (1985). Psychology: Handmaiden to society. In S. Koch & D. E. Leary (Eds.), *A century of psychology* (pp. 880–891). New York: McGraw-Hill.

Branch, M. N. (1987). Behavior analysis: A conceptual and empirical base for behavior therapy. *Behavior Therapist, 10(4),* 79–84.

Brehm, J. W., & Cohen, A. R. (1962). *Explorations in cognitive dissonance.* New York: Wiley.

Brewin, C. R. (1989). Cognitive change processes in psychotherapy. *Psychological Review, 96,* 379–394.

Bruner, J. (1986). *Actual minds, possible worlds.* Cambridge, MA: Harvard University Press.

Bruner, J. (1992). Another look at new look 1. *American Psychologist, 47,* 780–783.

Bryson, S. E., Doan, B. D., & Pasquali, P. (1984). Sadder but wiser: A failure to demonstrate that mood influences judgements of control. *Canadian Journal of Behavioral Science, 16,* 107–119.

Burchard, J. D. (1987). Social policy and the role of the behavior analyst in the prevention of delinquent behavior. *Behavior Analyst, 10,* 83–88.

Burchill, S. A. L., & Stiles, W. B. (1988). Interactions of depressed college students with their roommates: Not necessarily negative. *Journal of Personality and Social Psychology, 55,* 410–419.

Burton, L. M. (1990). Teenage childbearing as an alternative life-course strategy in multigeneration Black families. *Human Nature, 1,* 123–143.

Buss, A. R. (1975). The emerging field of the sociology of psychological knowledge. *American Psychologist, 30,* 988–1002.

Cacioppo, J. T., & Berntson, G. G. (1992). Social psychological contributions to the decade of the brain. *American Psychologist, 47,* 1019–1028.

Cacioppo, J. T., Berntson, G. G., & Andersen, B. L. (1991). Psychophysiological approaches to the evaluation of psychotherapeutic process and outcome, 1991: Contributions from social psychology. *Psychological Assessment, 3,* 321–336.

Cacioppo, J. T., & Petty, R. E. (1981). Electromyograms as measures of extent and affectivity of information processing. *American Psychologist, 36,* 441–456.

Cacioppo, J. T., & Petty, R. E. (Eds.). (1983). *Social psychophysiology: A sourcebook.* New York: Guilford.

Cacioppo, J. T., Petty, R. E., & Morris, K. J. (1985). Semantic, evaluative, and self-referent processing: Memory, cognitive effort, and somatovisceral activity. *Psychophysiology, 22,* 371–384.

Cacioppo, J. T., Petty, R. E., & Tassinary, L. G. (1989). Social psychophysiology: A new look. *Advances in Experimental Social Psychology, 22,* 39–91.

Cacioppo, J. T., Priester, R., & Berntson, G. G. (1993). Rudimentary determinants of attitudes. II: Arm flexion and extension have differential effects on attitudes. *Journal of Personality and Social Psychology, 65,* 5–17.

Cacioppo, J. T., & Tassinary, L. G. (1990). Inferring psychological significance from physiological signals. *American Psychologist, 45,* 16–28.

Campbell, K. (1970). *Body and mind.* London: Macmillan.

Cappella, J. N. (1981). Mutual influence in expressive behavior: Adult–adult and infant–adult dyadic interaction. *Psychological Bulletin, 89,* 101–132.

Carr, E. G. (1993). Behavior analysis is not ultimately about behavior. *Behavior Analyst, 16,* 47–49.

Cervone, D. (1985). Randomization tests to determine significance levels for microanalytic congruences between self-efficacy and behavior. *Cognitive Therapy and Research, 9,* 357–365.

Chabrol, H., Barrere, M., Guell, B. A., & Moron, P. (1986). Hyperfrontality of cerebral blood flow in depressed adolescents. *American Journal of Psychiatry, 143,* 263–264.

Chalmers, A. F. (1982). *What is this thing called science?* St. Lucia, Australia: University of Queensland Press.

Christensen-Szalanski, J. J. J., & Beach, L. R. (1984). The citation bias: Fad and fashion in the judgment and decision literature. *American Psychologist, 39,* 1400–1401.

Church, A. T., Teresa, J. S., Rosebrook, R., & Szendre, D. (1992). Self-efficacy for careers and occupational consideration in minority high school equivalency students. *Journal of Counseling Psychology, 39,* 498–508.

Clark, D. M. (1983). On the induction of depressed mood in the laboratory: Evaluation and comparison of the Velten and musical procedures. *Advances in Behaviour Research and Therapy, 5,* 27–49.

Clark, M. M., Abrams, D. B., Niaura, R. S., Eaton, C. A., & Rossi, J. S. (1991). Self-efficacy in weight management. *Journal of Consulting and Clinical Psychology, 59,* 739–744.

Condiotte, M. M., & Lichtenstein, E. (1981). Self-efficacy and relapse in smoking cessation programs. *Journal of Consulting and Clinical Psychology, 49,* 648–658.

Condon, W. S., & Ogston, W. D. (1966). Sound film analysis of normal and pathological behavior patterns. *Journal of Nervous and Mental Disease, 143,* 338–347.

Condon, W. S., & Sander, L. W. (1974). Synchrony demonstrated between movements of the neonate and adult speech. *Child Development, 45,* 456–462.

Corrigan, P. W. (1990). Theoretical weakness in behavior therapy is no more than statistical variance: A response to Christina Lee. *Journal of Behavior Therapy and Experimental Psychiatry, 21,* 141–142.

Costall, A. (1991). 'Graceful degradation': Cognitivism and the metaphors of the computer. In A. Still & A. Costall (Eds.), *Against cognitivism: Alternative foundations for cognitive psychology* (pp. 152–169). New York: Harvester Wheatsheaf.

Coyne, J. C. (1982). A critique of cognitions as causal entities with particular reference to depression. *Cognitive Therapy and Research, 6,* 1–13.

Coyne, J. C. (1994). Self-reported distress: Analog or ersatz depression? *Psychological Bulletin, 116,* 29–45.

Coyne, J. C., & Gotlib, I. (1986). Studying the role of cognition in depression: Well-trodden paths and cul-de-sacs. *Cognitive Therapy and Research, 10,* 695–705.

Craighead, W. E. (1990). There's a place for us: All of us. *Behavior Therapy, 21,* 3–23.

Cramer, D., & Fong, J. (1991). Effect of rational and irrational beliefs on intensity and "appropriateness" of feelings: A test of rational –emotive therapy. *Cognitive Therapy and Research, 15,* 319–329.

Cramer, D., & Kupshik, G. (1993). Effect of rational and irrational statements on intensity and "inappropriateness" of emotional distress and irrational beliefs in psychotherapy patients. *British Journal of Clinical Psychology, 32,* 319–325.

Crawford, R. (1977). You are dangerous to your health: The ideology and politics of victim blaming. *International Journal of Health Services, 7,* 663–680.

Cummings, K. M., Becker, M. H., & Maile, M. C. (1980). Bringing the models together: An empirical approach to combining variables used to explain health actions. *Journal of Behavioral Medicine, 3,* 123–145.

Davis, M. R. (1985). Perceptual and affective reverberation components. In A. B. Goldstein & G. Y. Michaels (Eds.), *Empathy: Development, training, and consequences* (pp. 62–108). Hillsdale, NJ: Lawrence Erlbaum Associates.

Delprato, D. J. (1993). Behavior analysis and S. C. Pepper's other mechanism. *Behavior Analyst, 16,* 51–53.

Dennard, D. O., & Hokanson, J. E. (1986). Performance on two cognitive tasks by dysphoric and nondysphoric students. *Cognitive Therapy and Research, 10,* 377–386.

Devins, G. M. (1992). Social cognitive analysis of recovery from a lapse after smoking cessation: Comment on Haaga and Stewart (1992). *Journal of Consulting and Clinical Psychology, 60,* 29 –31.

Dewberry, C., Ing, M., James, S., Nixon, M., & Richardson, S. (1990). Anxiety and unrealistic optimism. *Journal of Social Psychology, 130,* 151–156.

Dewberry, C., & Richardson, S. (1990). Effect of anxiety on optimism. *Journal of Social Psychology, 130,* 731–738.

DiClemente, C. C. (1991). Self-efficacy and smoking cessation maintenance: A preliminary report. *Cognitive Therapy and Research, 5,* 175–187.

DiClemente, C. C., Prochaska, J. O., & Gibertini, M. (1985). Self-efficacy and the stages of self-change of smoking. *Cognitive Therapy and Research, 9,* 181–200.

DiGiuseppe, R. A., Miller, N. J., & Trexler, L. D. (1977). A review of rational–emotive psychotherapy outcome studies. *Counseling Psychologist, 7(1),* 64–72.

Dobson, K. S. (1989). A meta-analysis of the efficacy of cognitive therapy for depression. *Journal of Consulting and Clinical Psychology, 57,* 414–419.

Dobson, K. S., Beamish, M., & Taylor, J. (1992). Advances in behavior therapy: The changing face of AABT conventions. *Behavior Therapy, 23,* 483–491.

Dobson, K. S., & Franche, R. (1989). A conceptual and empirical review of the depressive realism hypothesis. *Canadian Journal of Behavioral Science, 21,* 417–433.

Dobson, K. S., & Pusch, D. (1995). A test of the depressive realism hypothesis in clinically depressed subjects. *Cognitive Therapy and Research, 19,* 179–194.

Dolinski, D., Gromski, W., & Zawisza, E. (1987). Unrealistic pessimism. *Journal of Social Psychology, 127,* 511–516.

Dörner, D., & Schaub, H. (1994). Errors in planning and decision-making and the nature of human information processing. *Applied Psychology: An International Review, 43,* 433–453.

DuCharme, K. A., & Brawley, L. R. (1995). Predicting the intentions and behavior of exercise initiates using two forms of self-efficacy. *Journal of Behavioral Medicine, 18,* 479–497.

Duclos, S. E., Laird, J. D., Schneider, E., Sexter, M., Stern, L., & Van Lighten, O. (1989). Emotion-specific effects of facial expressions and postures on emotional experience. *Journal of Personality and Social Psychology, 57,* 100–108.

Duffy, R. E. (1934). Emotion: An example of the need for reorientation in psychology. *Psychological Review, 41,* 184–198.

Dumas, J. E. (1989). Let's not forget the context in behavioral assessment. *Behavioral Assessment, 11,* 231–247.

Dzewaltowski, D. A. (1989). Toward a model of exercise motivation. *Journal of Sport and Exercise Psychology, 11,* 251–269.

Dzewaltowski, D. A., Noble, J. M., & Shaw, J. M. (1990). Physical activity participation: Social cognitive theory versus the theories of reasoned action and planned behavior. *Journal of Sport and Exercise Psychology, 12,* 388–405.

Eastman, C., & Marzillier, J. S. (1984). Theoretical and methodological difficulties in Bandura's self-efficacy theory. *Cognitive Therapy and Research, 8,* 213–229.

Eden, D., & Zuk, Y. (1995). Seasickness as a self-fulfilling prophecy: Raising self-efficacy to boost performance at sea. *Journal of Applied Psychology, 80,* 628–635.

Eifert, G. H. (1985, May). *The use of music in counter-conditioning phobias: Clinical data and implications for conceptualizing the interplay between affect, behaviour, and cognition.* Paper presented at the Eighth National Conference of the Australian Behaviour Modification Association, Melbourne, Australia.

Eifert, G. H., Forsyth, J. P., & Schauss, S. L. (1993). Unifying the field: Developing an integrative paradigm for behavior therapy. *Journal of Behavior Therapy and Experimental Psychiatry, 24,* 107–118.

Eifert, G. H., & Plaud, J. J. (1993). From behavior theory to behavior therapy: The contributions of behavioral theories and research to the advancement of behavior therapy. *Journal of Behavior Therapy and Experimental Psychiatry, 24,* 101–105.

Eisenberger, R. (1992). Learned industriousness. *Psychological Review, 99,* 248–267.

Eiser, J. R. (1994). Risk judgements reflect belief strength, not bias. *Psychology and Health, 9,* 197–199.

Ekman, P. (1993). Facial expression and emotion. *American Psychologist, 48,* 384–392.

Ekman, P., Levenson, R. W., & Friesen, W. V. (1983). Autonomic nervous system activity distinguishes among emotions. *Science, 221,* 1208–1210.

Ellis, A. (1962). *Reason and emotion in psychotherapy.* New York: Lyle Stuart Press.

Ellis, A. (1977). Rejoinder: Elegant and inelegant RET. *Counseling Psychologist, 1(1),* 73–82.

Ellis, A. (1984). The essence of RET—1984. *Journal of Rational Emotive Therapy, 2(1),* 19–25.

Ellis, A. (1987). A sadly neglected cognitive element in depression. *Cognitive Therapy and Research, 11,* 121–146.

Ellis, A. (1993). Reflections on rational–emotive therapy. *Journal of Consulting and Clinical Psychology, 61,* 199–201.

Engels, G. I., Garnefski, N., & Diekstra, R. F. W. (1993). Efficacy of rational–emotive therapy: A quantitative analysis. *Journal of Consulting and Clinical Psychology, 61,* 1083–1090.

Epstein, R., Kirshnit, C. E., Lanza, R. P., & Rubin, L. C. (1984). "Insight" in the pigeon: Antecedents and determinants of an intelligent performance. *Nature, 308(5954),* 61–62.

Epstein, S. (1994). Integration of the cognitive and psychodynamic unconscious. *American Psychologist, 49,* 709–724.

Eriksen, C. W. (1960). Discrimination and learning without awareness: A methodological survey and evaluation. *Psychological Review, 67,* 279–300.

Erwin, E. (1992). Current philosophical issues in the scientific evaluation of behavior therapy theory and outcome. *Behavior Therapy, 23,* 151–172.

Eschenroeder, C. (1982). How rational is rational–emotive therapy? A critical appraisal of its theoretical foundations. *Cognitive Therapy and Research, 6,* 381–391.

Eysenck, H. J. (1978). Expectations as causal elements in behaviour change. *Advances in Behaviour Research and Therapy, 1,* 171–175.

Feltz, D. L., & Mugno, D. A. (1983). A replication of the path analysis of the causal elements of Bandura's theory of self-efficacy and the influence of autonomic perception. *Journal of Sport Psychology, 5,* 263–277.

Ferster, C. B., & Skinner, B. F. (1957). *Schedules of reinforcement.* New York: Appleton-Century-Crofts.

Feske, U., & Chambless, D. M. (1995). Cognitive behavioral versus exposure only treatments for social phobia: A meta-analysis. *Behavior Therapy, 26,* 695–720.

Festinger, L. (1957). *A theory of cognitive dissonance.* New York: Row & Peterson.

Fishbein, M., & Ajzen, I. (1975). *Belief, attitude, intention and behavior: An introduction to theory and research.* Reading, MA: Addison-Wesley.

Fletcher, G. J. O. (1984). Psychology and common sense. *American Psychologist, 39,* 203–213.

Forgas, J. P. (1994). The role of emotion in social judgments: An introductory review and an Affect Infusion Model (AIM). *European Journal of Social Psychology, 24,* 1–24.

Freimuth, M. (1992). Is the best always preferred? *American Psychologist, 47,* 673–674.

Freud, S. (1962). *Two short accounts of psycho-analysis* (J. Strachey, Trans.) Harmondsworth, England: Pelican. (Original work published 1910)

Fridlund, A. J., Schwartz, G. E., & Fowler, S. C. (1984). Pattern recognition of self-reported emotional state from multiple-site facial EMG activity during affective imagery. *Psychophysiology, 21,* 622–637.

Frisch, D., & Jones, S. K. (1993). Assessing the accuracy of decisions. *Theory and Psychology, 3,* 115–135.

Fryer, D. H. (1941). Articulation in automatic mental work. *American Journal of Psychology, 54,* 504–517.

Garcia, M. E., & Schmitz, J. M. (1990). A fine-grained analysis of the role of self-efficacy in self-initiated attempts to quit smoking. *Journal of Consulting and Clinical Psychology, 58,* 317–322.

Gattuso, S. M., Litt, M. D., & Fitzgerald, T. E. (1992). Coping with gastrointestinal endoscopy: Self-efficacy enhancement and coping style. *Journal of Consulting and Clinical Psychology, 60,* 133–139.

George, T. R. (1994). Self-confidence and baseball performance: A causal examination of self-efficacy theory. *Journal of Sport and Exercise Psychology, 16,* 381–399.

Gergen, K. J. (1989). Social psychology and the wrong revolution. *European Journal of Social Psychology, 19,* 463–484.

Geronimus, A. T. (1992). Clashes of common sense: On the previous child care experience of teenage mothers-to-be. *Human Organization, 51,* 318–329.

Gist, M. E., Schwoerer, C., & Rosen, B. (1989). Effects of alternative training methods on self-efficacy and performance in computer software training. *Journal of Applied Psychology, 74,* 884–891.

Glieck, J. (1987). *Chaos.* London: Heinemann.

Godding, P. R., & Glasgow, R. E. (1985). Self-efficacy and outcome expectations as predictors of controlled smoking status. *Cognitive Therapy and Research, 9,* 583–590.

Godin, G. (1993). The theories of reasoned action and planned behavior: Overview of findings, emerging research problems and usefulness for exercise promotion. *Journal of Applied Sport Psychology, 5,* 141–157.

Goffman, E. (1961). *On the characteristics of total institutions.* London: Houghton Mifflin.

Golin, S., Terrell, F., Weitz, J., & Drost, P. L. (1979). The illusion of control among depressed patients. *Journal of Abnormal Psychology, 88,* 454–457.

Gossette, R. L., & O'Brien, R. M. (1992). The efficacy of rational emotive therapy in adults: Clinical fact or psychometric artifact? *Journal of Behavior Therapy and Experimental Psychiatry, 23,* 9–24.

Gossette, R. L., & O'Brien, R. M. (1993). Efficacy of rational emotive therapy (RET) with children: A critical reappraisal. *Journal of Behavior Therapy and Experimental Psychiatry, 24,* 15–26.

Gotlib, I. H., & Meltzer, S. J. (1987). Depression and the perception of social skill in dyadic interaction. *Cognitive Therapy and Research, 11,* 41–54.

Gotlib, I. H., & Robinson, L. A. (1982). Responses to depressed individuals: Discrepancies between self-report and observer-rated behavior. *Journal of Abnormal Psychology, 91,* 231–240.

Granberg, D., & Brown, T. A. (1989). On affect and cognition in politics. *Social Psychology Quarterly, 52,* 171–182.

Greenberg, L. S., & Safran, J. D. (1984). Integrating affect and cognition: A perspective on the process of therapeutic change. *Cognitive Therapy and Research, 8,* 559–578.

Greenwald, A. G. (1992). New look 3: Unconscious cognition reclaimed. *American Psychologist, 47,* 766–780.

Greenwald, A. G., Pratkanis, A. R., Leippe, M. R., & Baumgardner, M. H. (1986). Under what conditions does theory obstruct research progress? *Psychological Review, 93,* 216–229.

Guidano, V. F., & Liotti, G. (1983). *Cognitive processes and emotional disorders.* New York: Guilford.

Haaga, D. A. F., & Beck, A. T. (1995). Perspectives on depressive realism: Implications for cognitive theory of depression. *Behaviour Research and Therapy, 33,* 41–48.

Haaga, D. A. F., & Davison, G. C. (1993). An appraisal of rational–emotive therapy. *Journal of Consulting and Clinical Psychology, 61,* 215–220.

Haaga, D. A. F., Dyck, M. J., & Ernst, D. (1991). Empirical status of cognitive theory of depression. *Psychological Bulletin, 110,* 215–236.

Haaga, D. A. F., & Stewart, B. L. (1992a). How do you know an act when you see one? A response to Devins (1992). *Journal of Consulting and Clinical Psychology, 60,* 32–33.

Haaga, D. A. F., & Stewart, B. L. (1992b). Self-efficacy for recovery from a lapse after smoking cessation. *Journal of Consulting and Clinical Psychology, 60,* 24–28.

Hackett, G. (1985). Role of mathematics self-efficacy in the choice of math-related majors of college women and men: A path analysis. *Journal of Counseling Psychology, 32,* 47–56.

Hackett, G., Betz, N., Casas, J. M., & Rocha-Singh, I. A. (1992). Gender, ethnicity, and social cognitive factors predicting the academic achievement of students in engineering. *Journal of Counseling Psychology, 39,* 527–538.

Hadar, U., Steiner, T. J., & Rose, F. C. (1985). Head movement during listening turns in conversation. *Journal of Nonverbal Behavior, 9,* 214–228.

Halasz, M. F. (1995). Nonlinear dynamics in behavioral systems. *American Psychologist, 50,* 107–108.

Hallam, R. S. (1987). Prospects for theoretical progress in behavior therapy. In H. J. Eysenck & I. Martin (Eds.), *Theoretical foundations of behavior therapy* (pp. 315–329). New York: Plenum.

Hatfield, E., Cacioppo, J. T., & Rapson, K. (1992). The logic of emotion: Emotional contagion. In M. S. Clark (Ed.), *Review of personality and social psychology* (pp. 151–177). Newbury Park, CA: Sage.

Hawkins, R. P. (1992). Self-efficacy: A predictor but not a cause of behavior. *Journal of Behavior Therapy and Experimental Psychiatry, 23,* 251–256.

Hawkins, R. P., Kashden, J., Hansen, D. J., & Sadd, D. L. (1992). The increasing reference to 'cognitive' variables in Behavior Therapy: A 20-year empirical analysis. *Behavior Therapist, 15,* 115–118.

Hayes, D. P., & Cobb, L. (1982). Cycles of spontaneous conversation under longterm isolation. In M. Davis (Ed.), *Interaction rhythms: Periodicity in communicative behavior* (pp. 319–340). New York: Human Sciences Press.

Hayes, S. C., & Hayes, L. J. (1992). Verbal relations and the evolution of behavior analysis. *American Psychologist, 47,* 1383–1395.

Hayes, S. C., Rincover, A., & Solnick, J. V. (1980). The technical drift of applied behavior analysis. *Journal of Applied Behavior Analysis, 13,* 275–285.

Hechtman, L. (1989). Teenage mothers and their children: Risks and problems: A review. *Canadian Journal of Psychiatry, 34,* 569–575.

Heider, F. (1944). Social perception and phenomenal causality. *Psychological Review, 51,* 358–374.

Heine, S. J., & Lehman, D. R. (1995). Cultural variation in unrealistic optimism: Does the west feel more invulnerable than the east? *Journal of Personality and Social Psychology, 68,* 595–607.

Hergenhahn, B. R. (1994). Psychology's cognitive revolution. *American Psychologist, 49,* 816–817.

Hess, U., & Kleck, R. E. (1990). Differentiating emotion elicited and deliberate emotional facial expressions. *European Journal of Social Psychology, 20,* 369–386.

Hickey, P. (1994). Resistance to behaviorism. *Behavior Therapist, 17,* 150–152.

Hilgard, E. R. (1986). *Divided consciousness: Multiple controls in human thought and action (expanded edition).* New York: Wiley.

Hineline, P. N. (1992). A self-interpretive behavior analysis. *American Psychologist, 47,* 1274–1286.

Hirst, W., & Gazzaniga, M. S. (1988). Present and future of memory research and its applications. In M. S. Gazzaniga (Ed.), *Perspectives in memory research* (pp. 275–308). Cambridge, MA: MIT Press.

Hogarth, R. M. (1981). Beyond discrete biases: Functional and dysfunctional aspects of judgmental heuristics. *Psychological Bulletin, 90,* 197–217.

Holahan, C. K., Holahan, C. J., & Belk, S. S. (1984). Adjustment in aging: The roles of life stresses, hassles, and self-efficacy. *Health Psychology, 3,* 315–328.

Holland, J. G. (1978). Behaviorism: Part of the problem or part of the solution? *Journal of Applied Behavior Analysis, 11,* 163–174.

Hollon, S. D., & Beck, A. T. (1979). Cognitive therapy of depression. In P. C. Kendall & S. D. Hollon (Eds.), *Cognitive behavioral interventions: Theory, research and procedures* (pp. 153–196). New York: Academic Press.

Holt, J., & Lee, C. (1989). Cognitive behaviour therapy re-examined: Problems and implications. *Australian Psychologist, 24,* 157–169.

Hope, D. A., Rapee, R. M., Heimberg, R. G., & Dombeck, M. J. (1990). Representations of the self in social phobia: Vulnerability to social threat. *Cognitive Therapy and Research, 14,* 177–189.

Howard, G. S. (1985). The role of values in the science of psychology. *American Psychologist, 40,* 255–265.

Howes, M. J., & Hokanson, J. E. (1979). Conversational and social responses to depressive interpersonal behavior. *Journal of Abnormal Psychology, 88,* 625–634.

Izard, C. E. (1977). *Human emotions.* New York: Plenum.

Jacoby, L. L., Toth, J. P., Lindsay, D. S., & Debner, J. A. (1992). Lectures for a layperson: Methods for revealing unconscious processes. In R. F. Bornstein & T. S. Pittman (Eds.), *Perception without awareness: Cognitive, clinical, and social perspectives* (pp. 81–120). New York: Guilford.

Jaeger, M. E., & Rosnow, R. L. (1988). Contextualism and its implications for psychological inquiry. *British Journal of Psychology, 79,* 63–75.

Jahoda, G. (1988). J'accuse. In M. H. Bond (Ed.), *The cross-cultural challenge to social psychology* (pp. 86–95). Los Angeles, CA: Sage.

James, W. (1893). *Psychology.* New York: Holt.

Janz, N. K., & Becker, M. H. (1984). The health belief model: A decade later. *Health Education Quarterly, 11,* 1–47.

Jason, L. A., & Glenwick, D. S. (1984). Behavioral community psychology: A review of recent research and applications. *Progress in Behavior Modification, 18,* 85–121.

Jaspars, J., Fincham, F. D., & Hewstone, M. (Eds.). (1983). *Attribution theory and research: Conceptual, developmental and social dimensions.* London: Academic Press.

Jemmott, J. B., Jemmott, L. S., Spears, H., Hewitt, N., & Cruz-Collins, M. (1992). Self-efficacy, hedonistic expectancies, and condom-use intentions among inner-city black adolescent women: A social cognitive approach to AIDS risk behavior. *Journal of Adolescent Health, 13,* 512–519.

Kahneman, D., Slovic, P., & Tversky, A. (1982). *Intuitive prediction: Biases and corrective procedures.* New York: Cambridge University Press.

Kahneman, D., & Tversky, A. (1973). On the psychology of prediction. *Psychological Review, 80,* 237–251.

Kaplan, R. M., Ries, A. L., Prewitt, L. M., & Eakin, E. (1994). Self-efficacy expectations predict survival for patients with chronic obstructive pulmonary disease. *Health Psychology, 13,* 366–368.

Kappas, A., Hess, U., & Scherer, K. R. (1991). Voice and emotion. In R. S. Feldman & B. Rime (Eds.), *Fundamentals of nonverbal behavior* (pp. 200–238). Cambridge, England: Cambridge University Press.

Kashima, Y., Siegal, M., Tanaka, K., & Kashima, E. S. (1992). Do people believe behaviours are consistent with attitudes? Towards a cultural psychology of attribution processes. *British Journal of Social Psychology, 31,* 111–124.

Katz, R. C., Stout, A., Taylor, C. B., Horne, M., & Agras, W. S. (1983). The contribution of arousal and performance in reducing spider avoidance. *Behavioral Psychotherapy, 11,* 127–138.

Kavanagh, D. J., & Bower, G. H. (1985). Mood and self-efficacy: Impact of joy and sadness on perceived capabilities. *Cognitive Therapy and Research, 9,* 507–526.

Kavanagh, D. J., Pierce, J., Lo, S. K., & Shelley, J. (1993). Self-efficacy and social support as predictors of smoking after a quit attempt. *Psychology and Health, 8,* 231–242.

Kazdin, A. E. (1978). Conceptual and assessment issues raised by self-efficacy theory. *Advances in Behaviour Research and Therapy, 1,* 177–185.

Kelley, H. H. (1992). Common-sense psychology and scientific psychology. *Annual Review of Psychology, 43,* 1–23.

Kendall, P. C. (1992). Healthy thinking. *Behavior Therapy, 23,* 1–11.

Kendall, P. C., Haaga, D. A. F., Ellis, A., Bernard, M., DiGuiseppe, R., & Kassinove, H. (1995). Rational–emotive therapy in the 1990s and beyond: Current status, recent revisions, and research questions. *Clinical Psychology Review, 15,* 169–185.

Kendall, P. C., & Korgeski, G. P. (1979). Assessment and cognitive–behavioral interventions. *Cognitive Therapy and Research, 3,* 1–21.

Kendler, H. H. (1993). Psychology and the ethics of social policy. *American Psychologist, 48,* 1046–1053.

Kendon, A. (1970). Movement coordination in social interaction: Some examples described. *Acta Psychologica, 32,* 100–125.

Kihlstrom, J. F., Barnhardt, T. M., & Tataryn, D.J. (1992a). Implicit perception. In R.F. Bornstein & T.S. Pittman (Eds.), *Perception without awareness: Cognitive, clinical, and social perspectives* (pp. 17 –54). New York: Guilford.

Kihlstrom, J. F., Barnhardt, T. M., & Tataryn, D. J. (1992b). The psychological unconscious: Found, lost, and regained. *American Psychologist, 47,* 788–791.

Kimble, G. A. (1989). Psychology from the standpoint of the generalist. *American Psychologist, 44,* 491–499.

Kimiecik, J. (1992). Predicting vigorous physical activity of corporate employees: Comparing the theories of reasoned action and planned behavior. *Journal of Sport and Exercise Psychology, 14,* 192–206.

Kipnis, D. (1994). Accounting for the use of behavior technologies in social psychology. *American Psychologist, 49,* 165–172.

Kirsch, I. (1986). Early research on self-efficacy: What we already know without knowing we know. *Journal of Social and Clinical Psychology, 4,* 339–358.

Kleck, R. E., Vaughan, R. C., Cartwright-Smith, J., Vaughan, K. B., Colby, C. Z., & Lanzetta, J. T. (1976). Effects of being observed on expressive, subjective, and physiological...

Krane, V., Williams, J., & Feltz, D. (1992). Path analysis examining relationships among cognitive anxiety, somatic anxiety, state confidence, performance expectations, and goal performance. *Journal of Sport Behavior, 15,* 279–296.

Kristiansen, C. M. (1987). Social learning theory and preventive health behaviour: Some neglected variables. *Social Behaviour, 2,* 73–86.

Kruglanski, A. W., & Klar, Y. (1985). Knowing what to do: On the epistemology of actions. In J. Kuhl & J. Beckmann (Eds.), *Action control: From cognition to behavior* (pp. 41–60). Berlin: Springer Verlag.

Kuhl, J. (1985). Volitional mediators of cognition–behavior consistency: Self-regulatory processes and action versus state orientation. In J. Kuhl & J. Beckmann (Eds.), *Action control: From cognition to behavior* (pp. 101–128). Berlin: Springer Verlag.

Kuhl, J., & Beckmann, J. (1985). Introduction and overview. In J. Kuhl & J. Beckmann (Eds.), *Action control: From cognition to behavior* (pp. 1–8). Berlin: Springer Verlag.

Kuiper, N. A., & MacDonald, M. R. (1982). Self and other perceptions in mild depressives. *Social Cognition, 1,* 223–239.

Kuiper, N. A., & MacDonald, M. R. (1983). Reason, emotion, and cognitive therapy. *Clinical Psychology Review, 3,* 297–316.

Kunda, Z. (1990). The case for motivated reasoning. *Psychological Bulletin, 108,* 480–498.

Kunst-Wilson, W. R., & Zajonc, R. B. (1980). Affective discrimination of stimuli that cannot be recognised. *Science, 207,* 557–558.

LaFrance, M. (1982). Posture mirroring and rapport. In M. Davis (Ed.), *Interaction rhythms* (pp. 279–297). New York: Human Sciences Press.

Laird, J. D. (1974). Self-attribution of emotion: The effects of expressive behavior on the quality of emotional experience. *Journal of Personality and Social Psychology, 29,* 475–486.

Laird, J. D., Wagener, J. J., Halal, M., & Szegda, M. (1982). Remembering what you feel: Effects of emotion on memory. *Journal of Personality and Social Psychology, 42,* 646–657.

Lakatos, I. (1978). *Philosophical papers* (J. Worrall & G. Currie, Eds.). Cambridge, England: Cambridge University Press.

Lamal, P. A. (1989). The impact of behaviorism on our culture: Some evidence and conjectures. *Psychological Record, 39,* 529–535.

Lang, P. J. (1978). Self-efficacy theory: Thoughts on cognition and unification. *Advances in Behaviour Research and Therapy, 1,* 187–192.

Langer, E. J. (1975). The illusion of control. *Journal of Personality and Social Psychology, 32,* 311–328.

Lanzetta, J. T., Cartwright-Smith, J., & Kleck, R. E. (1976). Effects of nonverbal dissimulation on emotional experience and autonomic arousal. *Journal of Personality and Social Psychology, 33,* 354–370.

Lapan, R. T., Boggs, K. R., & Morrill, W. H. (1989). Self-efficacy as a mediator of investigative and realistic general occupational themes on the Strong-Campbell Interest Inventory. *Journal of Counseling Psychology, 36,* 176–182.

Latimer, P. R., & Sweet, A. A. (1984). Cognitive versus behavioral procedures in cognitive–behavior therapy: A critical review of the evidence. *Journal of Behavior Therapy and Experimental Psychiatry, 15,* 9–22.

Lauver, P. J., & Jones, R. M. (1991). Factors associated with perceived career options in American Indian, white, and hispanic rural high school students. *Journal of Counseling Psychology, 38,* 159–166.

Lavy, E., van Oppen, P., & van den Hout, M. (1994). Selective processing of emotional information in obsessive compulsive disorder. *Behaviour Research and Therapy, 32,* 243–246.

Layne, C. (1983). Painful truths about depressives' cognitions. *Journal of Clinical Psychology, 39,* 848–853.

Leary, M. R., & Atherton, S. C. (1986). Self-efficacy, social anxiety, and inhibition in interpersonal encounters. *Journal of Social and Clinical Psychology, 4,* 256–267.

LeDoux, J. E. (1995). Emotion: Clues from the brain. *Annual Review of Psychology, 46,* 209–235.

Ledwidge, B. (1978). Cognitive behavior modification: A step in the wrong direction? *Psychological Bulletin, 85,* 353–375.

Lee, C. (1982). Self-efficacy as a predictor of performance in competitive gymnastics. *Journal of Sport Psychology, 4,* 404–409.

Lee, C. (1983). Self-efficacy and behaviour as predictors of subsequent behaviour in an assertiveness training programme. *Behaviour Research and Therapy, 21,* 225–232.

Lee, C. (1984a). Efficacy expectations and outcome expectations as predictors of performance in a snake-handling task. *Cognitive Therapy and Research, 8,* 509–516.

Lee, C. (1984b). The relative predictive accuracy of efficacy and outcome expectations in a simulated assertiveness task. *Cognitive Therapy and Research, 8,* 37–48.

Lee, C. (1987). Affective behaviour modification: A case for empirical investigation. *Journal of Behavior Therapy and Experimental Psychiatry, 18,* 203–213.

Lee, C. (1989a). Perceptions of immunity to disease in adult smokers. *Journal of Behavioral Medicine, 12,* 267–277.

Lee, C. (1989b). Theoretical problems lead to practical difficulties: The example of self-efficacy theory. *Journal of Behavior Therapy and Experimental Psychiatry, 20,* 115–123.

Lee, C. (1990). Theoretical weaknesses: Fundamental flaws in cognitive –behavioral theories are more than a problem of probability. *Journal of Behavior Therapy and Experimental Psychiatry, 21,* 143–145.

Lee, C. (1992). On cognitive theories and causation in human behavior. *Journal of Behavior Therapy and Experimental Psychiatry, 23,* 257–268.

Lee, C. (1993). Cognitive theory and therapy: Distinguishing psychology from ideology. *Australian Psychologist, 28,* 156–160.

Lee, C., & Bobko, P. (1994). Self-efficacy beliefs: Comparison of five measures. *Journal of Applied Psychology, 79,* 364–369.

Lee, V. L. (1993) Beyond the illusion of a mechanistic psychology. *Behavior Analyst, 16,* 55–58.

Leitenberg, M., Agras, W. S., Butz, R., & Wincze, J. (1971). Relationship between heart rate and behavioral change during the treatment of phobias. *Journal of Abnormal Psychology, 78,* 59–68.

Lent, R. W., Lopez, F. G., & Bieschke, K. J. (1991). Mathematics self-efficacy: Sources and relation to science-based career choice. *Journal of Counseling Psychology, 38,* 424–430.

Lerner, B. S., & Locke, E. A. (1995). The effects of goal setting, self-efficacy, competition, and personal traits on the performance of an endurance task. *Journal of Sport and Exercise Psychology, 17,* 138–152.

Leventhal, H., & Mosbach, P. A. (1983). The perceptual-motor theory of emotion. In J. T. Cacioppo & R. E. Petty (Eds.), *Social psychophysiology: A sourcebook* (pp. 353–386). New York: Guilford.

Levey, A. B., & Martin, I. (1983a). Cognitions, evaluations, and conditioning. *Advances in Behaviour Research and Therapy, 4,* 181–195.

Levey, A. B., & Martin, I. (1983b). Reply to comments on 'Cognitions, evaluations, and conditioning.' *Advances in Behaviour Research and Therapy, 4,* 219–223.

Lewicki, P., Hill, T., & Czyzewska, M. (1992). Nonconscious acquisition of information. *American Psychologist, 47,* 796–801.

Lewinsohn, P. M., Hoberman, H., Teri, L., & Hautzinger, M. (1985). An integrative theory of depression. In S. Reiss (Ed.), *Theoretical issues in behavior therapy* (pp. 331–359). New York: Academic Press.

Lewinsohn, P. M., Mischel, W., Chaplin, W., & Barton, R. (1980). Social competence and depression: The role of illusory self-perceptions. *Journal of Abnormal Psychology, 90,* 213–219.

Lewinsohn, P. M., Steinmetz, J. L., Larson, D. W., & Franklin, J. (1981). Depression-related cognitions: Antecedent or consequence? *Journal of Abnormal Psychology, 90,* 213–219.

Locke, E. A. (1994). The emperor is naked. *Applied Psychology: An International Review, 43,* 367–370.

Loewenstein, G., & Furstenberg, F. (1991). Is teenage sexual behavior rational? *Journal of Applied Social Psychology, 21,* 957 –986.

Loken, B., & Fishbein, M. (1980). An analysis of the effects of occupational variables on childbearing intentions. *Journal of Applied Social Psychology, 10,* 202–223.

Longo, D. A., Lent, R. W., & Brown, S. D. (1992). Social cognitive variables in the prediction of client motivation and attrition. *Journal of Counseling Psychology, 39,* 447–452.

Lopes, L. L. (1991). The rhetoric of irrationality. *Theory and Psychology, 1,* 65–82.

Luborsky, L., Singer, B., & Luborsky, L. (1975). Comparative studies of psychotherapies: Is it true that "everyone has won and all must have prizes"? *Archives of General Psychiatry, 32,* 995–1008.

Luzzo, D. A. (1993). Value of career-decision-making self-efficacy in predicting career-decision-making attitudes and skills. *Journal of Counseling Psychology, 40,* 194–199.

MacLeod, C. M. (1991). Half a century of research on the Stroop effect: An integrative review. *Psychological Bulletin, 109,* 163–203.

Mackie, D. M., & Worth, L. T. (1991). Feeling good but not thinking straight: The impact of positive mood on persuasion. In J. P. Forgas (Ed.), *Emotion and social judgments* (pp. 201–219). New York: Pergamon.

Maddux, J. E. (1993). Social cognitive models of health and exercise behavior: An introduction and review of conceptual issues. *Journal of Applied Sport Psychology, 5,* 116–140.

Maddux, J. E., Norton, L. W., & Stoltenberg, C. D. (1986). Self-efficacy expectancy, outcome expectancy, and outcome value: Relative effects on behavioral intentions. *Journal of Personality and Social Psychology, 51,* 783–789.

Maddux, J. E., & Rogers, R. W. (1983). Protection motivation and self-efficacy: A revised theory of fear appeals and attitude change. *Journal of Experimental Social Psychology, 19,* 469–479.

Maddux, J. E., Sherer, M., & Rogers, R. W. (1982). Self-efficacy expectancy and outcome expectancy: Their relationship and their effects on behavioral intentions. *Cognitive Therapy and Research, 6,* 207–211.

Maddux, J. E., & Stanley, M. A. (1986). Self-efficacy theory in contemporary psychology: An overview. *Journal of Social and Clinical Psychology, 4,* 249–255.

Mahoney, M. J. (1974). *Cognition and behavior modification.* Cambridge, MA: Ballinger.

Mahoney, M. J. (1977). A critical analysis of rational –emotive theory and therapy. *Counseling Psychologist, 7(1),* 44–46.

Malagodi, E. F. (1986). On radicalizing behaviorism: A call for cultural analysis. *Behavior Analyst, 9,* 1–17.

Malpass, R. S. (1988). Why not cross-cultural psychology: A characterisation of some mainstream views. In M. H. Bond (Ed.), *The cross-cultural challenge to social psychology* (pp. 29–35). Los Angeles, CA: Sage.

Mandel, D. R. (1995). Chaos theory, sensitive dependence, and the logistic equation. *American Psychologist, 50,* 106–107.

Marcus, B. H., & Owen, N. (1992). Motivational readiness, self-efficacy, and decision-making for exercise. *Journal of Applied Social Psychology, 22,* 3–16.

Marcus, D. K., & Nardone, M. E. (1992). Depression and interpersonal rejection. *Clinical Psychology Review, 12,* 433–449.

Markus, H. R., & Kitayama, S. (1991). Culture and the self: Implications for cognition, emotion, and motivation. *Psychological Bulletin, 98,* 224–253.

Marlatt, G. A., & Gordon, J. R. (Eds.). (1985). *Relapse prevention*. New York: Guilford.

Marr, M. J. (1993). Contextualistic mechanism or mechanistic contextualism? The straw machine as tar baby. *Behavior Analysis, 16,* 59–65.

Martin, D. J., Abramson, L. Y., & Alloy, L. B. (1984). Illusion of control for self and others in depressed and nondepressed college students. *Journal of Personality and Social Psychology, 46,* 125–136.

Martocchio, J. J. (1994). Effects of conceptions of ability on anxiety, self-efficacy, and learning in training. *Journal of Applied Psychology, 79,* 819–825.

Massey, G. J. (1993). Mind–body problems. *Journal of Sport and Exercise Psychology, 15,* S97–S115.

Mathews, A., & Klug, F. (1993). Emotionality and interference with color-naming in anxiety. *Behaviour Research and Therapy, 31,* 57–62.

Mathews, A., & MacLeod, C. (1985). Selective processing of threat cues in anxiety states. *Behaviour Research and Therapy, 23,* 563–569.

Matt, G. E., Vazquez, C., & Campbell, W. K. (1992). Mood-congruent recall of affectively toned stimuli: A meta-analytic review. *Clinical Psychology Review, 12,* 227–255.

McAuley, E. (1992). The role of efficacy cognitions in the prediction of exercise behavior in middle-aged adults. *Journal of Behavioral Medicine, 15,* 65–88.

McAuley, E. (1993). Self-efficacy and the maintenance of exercise participation in older adults. *Journal of Behavioral Medicine, 16,* 103–113.

McAuley, E., Courneya, K. S., & Lettunich, J. (1991). Effects of acute and long-term exercise on self-efficacy responses in sedentary, middle-aged males and females. *Gerontologist, 31,* 534–542.

McGaw, B. (1992). Testing in education. *Australian Psychologist, 27,* 1–11.

McGuigan, F. J. (1970). Covert oral behavior during the silent performance of language tasks. *Psychological Bulletin, 74,* 309–326.

McKenna, F. P. (1993). It won't happen to me: Unrealistic optimism or illusion of control? *British Journal of Psychology, 84,* 39–50.

Meichenbaum, D. H. (1974). *Cognitive behavior modification*. New York: Plenum.

Meichenbaum, D. H. (1977). Dr Ellis, please stand up. *Counseling Psychologist, 7(1),* 43–44.

Meichenbaum, D. H. (1993). Changing conceptions of cognitive behavior modification: Retrospect and prospect. *Journal of Consulting and Clinical Psychology, 61,* 202–204.

Meier, S. T. (1983). Toward a theory of burnout. *Human Relations, 36,* 899–910.

Merikle, P. M., & Reingold, E. M. (1992). Measuring unconscious perceptual processes. In R. F. Bornstein & T. S. Pittman (Eds.), *Perception without awareness: Cognitive, clinical, and social perspectives* (pp. 55–80). New York: Guilford.

Meyer, B. E. B., & Hokanson, J. E. (1985). Situational influences on social behaviors of depression-prone individuals. *Journal of Clinical Psychology, 41,* 29–35.

Michelson, L., & Mavissakalian, M. (1985). Psychophysiological outcome of behavioral and pharmacological treatments of agoraphobia. *Journal of Consulting and Clinical Psychology, 53,* 229–236.

Miller, M., Carlyle, S., & Pease, R. (1992). The relationship between motivation and self-efficacy in competitive athletes participating in swimming, ice hockey, and basketball. *Journal of Sport Behavior, 15,* 201–208.

Mineka, S. (1987). A primate model of phobic fears. In H. J. Eysenck & T. Martin (Eds.), *Theoretical foundations of behavior therapy* (pp. 81–111). New York: Plenum.

Mixon, D. (1991). On not-doing and on trying and failing. In A. Still & A. Costall (Eds.), *Against cognitivism: Alternative foundations for cognitive psychology* (pp. 28–37). New York: Harvester Wheatsheaf.

Modgil, S., & Modgil, C. (Eds.). (1987). *B. F. Skinner: Consensus and controversy*. New York: Falmer Press.

Moore, D. L., & Baron, R. S. (1983). Social facilitation: a psychophysiological analysis. In J. T. Cacioppo & R. E. Petty (Eds.), *Social psychophysiology: A sourcebook* (pp. 434–466). New York: Guilford.

Morf, M. E. (1994). Sperry's leap. *American Psychologist, 49,* 817–818.

Morris, E. K. (1988). Contextualism: The world view of behavior analysis. *Journal of Experimental Child Psychology, 46,* 289–323.

Morris, E. K. (1991). The contextualism that is behaviour analysis: An alternative to cognitive psychology. In A. Still & A. Costall (Eds.), *Against cognitivism: Alternative foundations for cognitive psychology* (pp. 12 –149). New York: Harvester Wheatsheaf.

Mudde, A. N., Kok, G., & Strecher, V. (1995). Self-efficacy as a predictor for the cessation of smoking: Methodological issues and implications for smoking cessation programs. *Psychology and Health, 10,* 353–367.

Mullen, P. D., Hersey, J. C., & Iverson, D. C. (1987). Health behavior models compared. *Social Science and Medicine, 24,* 973–981.

Multon, K. D., Brown, S. D., & Lent, R. W. (1990). Relation of self-efficacy beliefs to academic outcomes: A meta-analytic investigation. *Journal of Counseling Psychology, 38,* 30–38.

Munro, D. (1992). Process vs structure and levels of analysis in psychology: Towards integration rather than reduction of theories. *Theory and Psychology, 2,* 109–127.

Newman, M. G., Hofmann, S. G., Trabert, W., Roth, W. T., & Taylor, C. B. (1994). Does behavioral treatment of social phobia lead to cognitive changes? *Behavior Therapy, 25,* 503–517.

Nezlek, J. B., Imbrie, M., & Shean, G. D. (1994). Depression and everyday social interaction. *Journal of Personality and Social Psychology, 67,* 1101–1111.

Nisbett, R. E., Krantz, D. H., Jepson, C., & Kunda, Z. (1983). The use of statistical heuristics in everyday inductive reasoning. *Psychological Review, 90,* 339–363.

Nisbett, R. E., & Valins, S. (1971). Perceiving the causes of one's own behaviour. In E. E. Jones et al. (Eds.), *Attribution: Perceiving the causes of behavior* (pp. 63–78). New Jersey: General Learning Press.

Nisbett, R. E., & Wilson, T. D. (1977). Telling more than we can know: Verbal reports on mental processes. *Psychological Review, 84,* 231–256.

Norem, J. K., & Cantor, N. (1986). Defensive pessimism: Harnessing anxiety as motivation. *Journal of Personality and Social Psychology, 51,* 1208–1217.

Norman, D. A. (1981). Categorisation of action slips. *Psychological Review, 88,* 1–15.

Norman, P. (1991). Social learning theory and the prediction of attendance at screening. *Psychology and Health, 5,* 231–239.

Norman, P., & Conner, M. (1993). The role of social cognition models in predicting attendance at health checks. *Psychology and Health, 8,* 447–462.

Norman, P., & Smith, L. (1995). The theory of planned behaviour and exercise: An investigation into the role of prior behaviour, behavioural intentions and attitude variability. *European Journal of Social Psychology, 25,* 403–415.

Oei, T. P. S., Hansen, J., & Miller, S. (1993). The empirical status of irrational beliefs in rational emotive therapy. *Australian Psychologist, 28,* 195–200.

Öhman, A. (1988). Nonconscious control of autonomic responses: A role for Pavlovian conditioning? *Biological Psychology, 27,* 113–135.

Olinger, L. J., Kuiper, N. A., & Shaw, B. F. (1987). Dysfunctional attitudes and stressful life events: An interactive model of depression. *Cognitive Therapy and Research, 11,* 25–40.

Omer, H., & Dar, R. (1992). Changing trends in three decades of psychotherapy research: The flight from theory into pragmatics. *Journal of Consulting and Clinical Psychology, 60,* 88–93.

Padgett, D. K. (1991). Correlates of self-efficacy beliefs among patients with non-insulin dependent diabetes mellitus in Zagreb, Yugoslavia. *Patient Education and Counseling, 18,* 139–147.

Pajares, F., & Miller, M. D. (1995). Mathematics self-efficacy and mathematics performances: The need for specificity of assessment. *Journal of Counseling Psychology, 42,* 190–198.

Parker, L. E. (1994). Working together: Perceived self- and collective-efficacy at the workplace. *Journal of Applied Social Psychology, 24,* 43–59.

Parrott, W. G., & Sabini, J. (1989). On the 'emotional' qualities of certain types of cognition: A reply to arguments for the independence of cognition and affect. *Cognitive Therapy and Research, 13,* 49–65.

Pelham, B. W. (1991). On the benefits of misery: Self-serving biases in the depressive self-concept. *Journal of Personality and Social Psychology, 61,* 670–681.

Petty, R. E., Gleicher, F., & Baker, S. M. (1991). Multiple roles for affect in persuasion. In J. P. Forgas (Ed.), *Emotion and social judgments* (pp. 181–200). New York: Pergamon.

Plaud, J. J., & Vogeltanz, N. D. (1993). Behavior therapy and the experimental analysis of behavior: Contributions of the science of human behavior and radical behavioral philosophy. *Journal of Behavior Therapy and Experimental Psychiatry, 24,* 119–127.

Poag, K., & McAuley, E. (1992). Goal-setting, self-efficacy, and exercise behavior. *Journal of Sport Psychology, 14,* 352–360.

Prilleltensky, I. (1989). Psychology and the status quo. *American Psychologist, 44,* 795–802.

Prilleltensky, I. (1990a). Enhancing the social ethics of psychology: Toward a psychology at the service of social change. *Canadian Psychology, 31,* 310–319.

Prilleltensky, I. (1990b). On the social and political implications of cognitive psychology. *Journal of Mind and Behavior, 11,* 127–136.

Prilleltensky, I. (1990c). The politics of abnormal psychology: Past, present and future. *Political Psychology, 11,* 767–785.

Prilleltensky, I. (1990d). Psychology in industry: Origins and sociopolitical implications. *Critical Sociology, 17(2),* 73–91.

Prilleltensky, I. (1992). Radical behaviorism and the social order. *Counseling and Values, 36,* 104–111.

Prilleltensky, I. (1994a). On the social legacy of B. F. Skinner: Rhetoric of change, philosophy of adjustment. *Theory and Psychology, 4,* 125–137.

Prilleltensky, I. (1994b). Psychology and social ethics. *American Psychologist, 49,* 966–967.

Quine, W. V. (1989). Mind, brain and behavior. In A. J. Brownstein (Ed.), *Progress in behavioral studies, Vol 1* (pp. 1–6). Hillsdale, NJ: Lawrence Erlbaum Associates.

Rachlin, H., Logue, A. W., Gibbon, J., & Frankel, M. (1986). Cognition and behavior in studies of choice. *Psychological Review, 93,* 33–45.

Rachman, S. (1980). Emotional processing. *Behaviour Research and Therapy, 18,* 51–60.

Rachman, S. (1981). The primacy of affect: Some theoretical implications. *Behaviour Research and Therapy, 19,* 279–290.

Rachman, S. (1983). Irrational thinking, with special reference to cognitive therapy. *Advances in Behaviour Research and Therapy, 5,* 63–88.

Rachman, S. (1984). A reassessment of the 'primacy of affect.' *Cognitive Therapy and Research, 8,* 579–584.

Rachman, S., & Hodgson, R. (1974). Synchrony and desynchrony in fear and avoidance. *Behaviour Research and Therapy, 12,* 311–318.

Rapee, R. M., McCallum, S. L., Melville, L. F., Ravenscroft, H., & Rodney, J. M. (1994). Memory bias in social phobia. *Behaviour Research and Therapy, 32,* 89–99.

Reason, J. (1977). Skill and error in everyday life. In M. J. Howe (Ed.), *Adult learning: Psychological research and applications* (pp. 21–44). New York: Wiley.

Reason, J. (1979). Actions not as planned: The price of automatization. In G. Underwood & R. Stevens (Eds.), *Aspects of consciousness* (pp. 67–89). London: Academic Press.

Reason, J. (1984). Lapses of attention in everyday life. In R. Parasuraman & D. R. Davies (Eds.), *Varieties of attention* (pp. 515–550). Orlando, FL: Academic Press.

Reason, J. (1990a). The contribution of latent human failures to the breakdown of complex systems. *Philosophical Transactions of the Royal Society of London, Series B, 327,* 475–484.

Reason, J. (1990b). The problem with automation: Inappropriate feedback and interaction, not 'over-automation.' *Philosophical Transactions of the Royal Society of London, Series B, 327,* 585–593.

Reason, J., & Lucas, D. (1984). Absent-mindedness in shops: Its incidence, correlates and consequences. *British Journal of Clinical Psychology, 23,* 121–131.

Reason, J., Manstead, A., Stradling, S., Baxter, J., & Campbell, K. (1990). Errors and violations on the roads: A real distinction? *Ergonomics, 33,* 1315–1332.

Rée, J. (1974). *Descartes*. London: Allen Lane.

Reisenzein, R. (1984). The Schachter theory of emotion: Two decades later. *Psychological Bulletin, 94,* 239–264.

Rime, B., & Schiaratura, L. (1991). Gesture and speech. In R. S. Feldman & B. Rime (Eds.), *Fundamentals of nonverbal behavior* (pp. 239–281). Cambridge, England: Cambridge University Press.

Riskind, J. H. (1984). They stoop to conquer: Guiding and self-regulatory functions of physical posture after success and failure. *Journal of Personality and Social Psychology, 47,* 479–493.

Robertson, L. C. (1987). A cognitive approach to behavior. In S. Modgil & C. Modgil (Eds.), *B. F. Skinner: Consensus and controversy* (pp. 295–305). New York: Falmer Press.

Robins, R. W., & Craik, K. H. (1993). Is there a citation bias in the judgment and decision literature? *Organizational Behavior and Human Decision Processes, 54,* 225–244.

Rogers, R. W. (1983). Cognitive and physiological processes in fear appeals and attitude change: A revised theory of protection motivation. In J. T. Cacioppo & R. E. Petty (Eds.), *Social psychophysiology: A sourcebook* (pp. 153–176). New York: Guilford.

Rogoff, B., & Chavajay, P. (1995). What's become of research on the cultural basis of cognitive development? *American Psychologist, 50,* 859–877.

Ronis, D. L. (1992). Conditional health threats: Health beliefs, decisions, and behaviors among adults. *Health Psychology, 11,* 127–135.

Rorer, L. G. (1989). Rational–emotive theory: I. An integrated psychological and philosophical basis. *Cognitive Therapy and Research, 13,* 475–492.

Rosenblatt, A., & Greenberg, J. (1991). Examining the world of the depressed: Do depressed people prefer others who are depressed? *Journal of Personality and Social Psychology, 60,* 620–629.

Rosenfarb, I. S., Burker, E. J., Morris, S. A., & Cush, D. T. (1993). Effects of changing contingencies on the behavior of depressed and nondepressed individuals. *Journal of Abnormal Psychology, 102,* 642–646.

Sadri, G., & Robertson, I. T. (1993). Self-efficacy and work-related behaviour: A review and meta-analysis. *International Journal of Applied Psychology, 42,* 139–152.

Salzinger, K. (1992). Cognitive therapy: A misunderstanding of B. F. Skinner. *Journal of Behavior Therapy and Experimental Psychiatry, 23,* 3–8.

Sampson, E. E. (1977). Psychology and the American ideal. *Journal of Personality and Social Psychology, 35,* 767–782

Sampson, E. E. (1981). Cognitive psychology as ideology. *American Psychologist, 36,* 730–743.

Sampson, E. E. (1988). The debate on individualism: Indigenous psychologies of the individual and their role in personal and social functioning. *American Psychologist, 43,* 15–22.

Sampson, E. E. (1991). The democratisation of psychology. *Theory and Psychology, 1,* 275–298.

Sampson, E. E. (1994). Sperry's cognitive revolution. *American Psychologist, 49,* 818–819.

Sanna, L. J. (1992). Self-efficacy theory: Implications for social facilitation and social loafing. *Journal of Personality and Social Psychology, 62,* 774–786.

Sarason, S. B. (1981). An asocial psychology and a misdirected clinical psychology. *American Psychologist, 36,* 827–836.

Sarver, V. T. (1983). Ajzen and Fishbein's 'Theory of reasoned action': A critical assessment. *Journal for the Theory of Social Behaviour, 13,* 155–163.

Scarr, S. (1985). Constructing psychology: Making facts and fables for our times. *American Psychologist, 40,* 499–512.

Scheier, M. F., & Carver, C. S. (1992). Effects of optimism on psychological and physical well-being: Theoretical overview and empirical update. *Cognitive Therapy and Research, 16,* 201–228.

Schiaffino, K. M., Revenson, T. A., & Gibofsky, A. (1991). Assessing the impact of self-efficacy beliefs on adaptation to rheumatoid arthritis. *Arthritis Care and Research, 4,* 150–157.

Schnaitter, R. (1987a). Behaviorism is not cognitive and cognitivism is not behavioral. *Behaviorism, 15,* 1–11.

Schnaitter, R. (1987b). Knowledge as action: The epistemology of radical behaviorism. In S. Modgil & C. Modgil (Eds.), *B. F. Skinner: Consensus and controversy* (pp. 57–68). New York: Falmer Press.

Schuster, H. G. (1989). *Deterministic chaos* (2nd ed.). Weinheim, Germany: VCH Verlagsgesellschaft.

Schwartz, G. E., Fair, P. L., Salt, P., Mandel, M. R., & Klerman, G. L. (1976). Facial expression and imagery in depression: An elctromyographic study. *Psychosomatic Medicine, 38*, 337–347.

Schwartz, G. E., Fair, P. L., Mandel, M. R., Salt, P., Mieske, M., & Klerman, G. L. (1978). Facial electromyography in the assessment of improvement in depression. *Psychosomatic Medicine, 40*, 355–360.

Schwarz, N. (1990). Assessing frequency reports of mundane behaviors: Contributions of cognitive psychology to questionnaire construction. *Review of Personality and Social Psychology, 11*, 98–119.

Schwarz, N., & Bless, H. (1991). Happy and mindless, but sad and smart? The impact of affective states on analytical reasoning. In J. P. Forgas (Ed.), *Emotion and social judgments* (pp. 59–71). New York: Pergamon.

Schwarz, N., Bless, H., & Bohner, G. (1991). Mood and persuasion: Affective states influence the processing of persuasive communications. *Advances in Experimental Social Psychology, 24*, 161–199.

Schwarzer, R. (1994). Optimism, vulnerability, and self-beliefs as health-related cognitions: A systematic overview. *Psychology and Health, 9*, 161–180.

Segal, Z. V., & Marshall, W. L. (1986). Discrepancies between self-efficacy predictions and actual performance in a population of rapists and child molesters. *Cognitive Therapy and Research, 10*, 363–375.

Segrin, C., & Abramson, L. Y. (1994). Negative reactions to depressive behaviors: A communication theories analysis. *Journal of Abnormal Psychology, 103*, 655–668.

Sellen, A. J. (1994). Detection of everyday errors. *Applied Psychology: An International Review, 43*, 475–498.

Sexton, T. L., Tuckman, B. W., & Crehan, K. (1992). An investigation of the patterns of self-efficacy, outcome expectation, outcome value, and performance across trials. *Cognitive Therapy and Research, 16*, 329–348.

Seydel, E., Taal, E., & Wiegman, O. (1990). Risk-appraisal, outcome and self-efficacy expectations: Cognitive factors in preventive behavior related to cancer. *Psychology and Health, 4*, 99–109.

Sharpe, P. A., & Connell, C. M. (1992). Exercise beliefs and behaviors among older employees: A health promotion trial. *The Gerontologist, 32*, 444–449.

Shaw, B. F. (1977). Comparison of cognitive therapy and behavior therapy in the treatment of depression. *Journal of Consulting and Clinical Psychology, 45*, 543–551.

Sheppard, B. H., Hartwick, J., & Warshaw, P. R. (1988). The theory of reasoned action: A meta-analysis of past research with recommendations for modifications and future research. *Journal of Consumer Research, 15*, 325–343.

Sherman, S. J. (1980). On the self-erasing nature of errors of prediction. *Journal of Personality and Social Psychology, 39*, 211–221.

Shull, R. L., & Lawrence, P. S. (1993). Is contextualism productive? *Behavior Analyst, 16*, 241–243.

Silver, W. S., Mitchell, T. R., & Gist, M. E. (1995). Responses to successful and unsuccessful performance: The moderating effect of self-efficacy on the relationship between performance and attributions. *Organizational Behavior and Human Decision Processes, 62,* 286–299.

Silverman, J. S., Silverman, J. A., & Eardley, D. A. (1984). Do maladaptive attitudes cause depression? *Archives of General Psychiatry, 41,* 28–30.

Skinner, B. F. (1953). *Science and human behavior.* New York: Macmillan.

Skinner, B. F. (1977). Why I am not a cognitive psychologist. *Behaviorism, 5,* 1–10.

Skinner, B. F. (1984). The shame of American education. *American Psychologist, 39,* 947–954.

Skinner, B. F. (1985). Toward the cause of peace: What can psychology contribute? *Applied Social Psychology Annual, 6,* 21–25.

Skinner, B. F. (1986). What is wrong with daily life in the Western world? *American Psychologist, 41,* 568–574.

Skinner, B. F. (1987). Whatever happened to psychology as the science of behavior? *American Psychologist, 42,* 780–786.

Skinner, B. F. (1989). The origins of cognitive thought. *American Psychologist, 44,* 13–18.

Skinner, B. F. (1990). Can psychology be a science of mind? *American Psychologist, 45,* 1206–1210.

Slovic, P. (1995). The construction of preference. *American Psychologist, 50,* 364–371.

Smith, E. R., & Miller, F. D. (1978). Limits on perception of cognitive processes: A reply to Nisbett and Wilson. *Psychological Review, 85,* 355–362.

Spence, J. T. (1985). Achievement American style. *American Psychologist, 40,* 1275–1295.

Sperry, R. (1993). The impact and promise of the cognitive revolution. *American Psychologist, 48,* 878–885.

Sperry, R. (1995). The future of psychology. *American Psychologist, 50,* 505–506.

Staats, A. W. (1989). Unificationism: Philosophy for the modern disunified science of psychology. *Philosophical Psychology, 2,* 143–164.

Staats, A. W. (1991). Unified positivism and unification psychology: Fad or new field? *American Psychologist, 46,* 899–912.

Staddon, J. E. R. (1984). Social learning theory and the dynamics of interaction. *Psychological Review, 91,* 502–507.

Staddon, J. E. R. (1993a). *Behaviorism.* London: Duckworth.

Staddon, J. E. R. (1993b). Pepper with a pinch of psalt. *Behavior Analyst, 16,* 245–250.

Still, A., & Costall, A. (Eds.). (1991). *Against cognitivism: Alternative foundations for cognitive psychology.* New York: Harvester Wheatsheaf.

Strack, S., & Coyne, J. C. (1983). Social confirmation of dysphoria: Shared and private reactions to depression. *Journal of Personality and Social Psychology, 44,* 798–806.

Swann, W. B., Stein-Seroussi, A., & Giesler, R. B. (1992). Why people self-verify. *Journal of Personality and Social Psychology, 62,* 392–401.

Swann, W. B., Wenzlaff, R. M., Krull, D. S., & Pelham, B. W. (1992). Allure of negative feedback: Self-verification strivings among depressed persons. *Journal of Abnormal Psychology, 101,* 293–306.

Sweet, A. (1994). Member says whoa! *Behavior Therapist, 17(2),* 44.

Tannenbaum, S. I., Mathieu, J. E., Salas, E., & Cannon-Bowers, J. A. (1991). Meeting trainees' expectations: The influence of training fulfilment on the development of commitment, self-efficacy, and motivation. *Journal of Applied Psychology, 76,* 759–769.

Taylor, J. (1989). The effects of personal and competitive self-efficacy and differential outcome feedback on subsequent self-efficacy and performance. *Cognitive Therapy and Research, 13,* 67–79.

Taylor, S. E., & Brown, J. D. (1988). Illusion and well-being: A social psychological perspective on mental health. *Psychological Bulletin, 103,* 193–210.

Taylor, S. E., & Gollwitzer, P. M. (1995). Effects of mindset on positive illusions. *Journal of Personality and Social Psychology, 69,* 213–226.

Tedesco, L. A., Keffer, M. A., Davis, E. L., & Christersson, L. A. (1993). Self-efficacy and reasoned action: Predicting oral health status and behavior at one, three and six month intervals. *Psychology and Health, 8,* 105–121.

Tedesco, L. A., Keffer, M. A., & Fleck-Kandath, C. (1991). Self-efficacy, reasoned action, and oral health behavior reports: A social cognitive approach to compliance. *Journal of Behavioral Medicine, 14,* 341–355.

Tickle-Degnen, L., & Rosenthal, R. (1987). Group rapport and nonverbal behavior. *Review of Personality and Social Psychology, 9,* 113–136.

Tom, G., Petterson, P., Lau, T., Burton, T., & Cook, J. (1991). The role of overt head movement in the formation of affect. *Basic and Applied Social Psychology, 12,* 281–289.

Triandis, H. C. (1980). Values, attitudes, and interpersonal behavior. In M. M. Page (Ed.), *Nebraska Symposium on Motivation 1979* (Vol. 27, pp. 195–259). Nebraska: University of Nebraska Press.

Tryon, W. W. (1981). A methodological critique of Bandura's self-efficacy theory of behavior change. *Journal of Behavior Therapy and Experimental Psychiatry, 12,* 113–114.

Tryon, W. W. (1982). Reinforcement history as a possible basis for the relationship between self-percepts of efficacy and responses to treatment. *Journal of Behavior Therapy and Experimental Psychiatry, 13,* 201–202.

Tsal, Y. (1985). On the relationship between cognitive and affective processes: A critique of Zajonc and Markus. *Journal of Consumer Research, 12,* 358–362.

Tulving, E. (1985). How many memory systems are there? *American Psychologist, 40,* 385–398.

Tversky, A., & Kahneman, D. (1981). The framing of decisions and the psychology of choice. *Science, 211,* 453–458.

Vallone, R. P., Griffin, D. W., Lin, S., & Ross, L. (1990). Overconfident prediction of future actions and outcomes by self and others. *Journal of Personality and Social Psychology, 58,* 582–592.

Vermilyea, J. A., Boice, R., & Barlow, D. H. (1984). Rachman and Hodgson (1974) a decade later: How do desynchronous response systems relate to the treatment of agoraphobia? *Behaviour Research and Therapy, 22,* 615–621.

Vestre, N. D., & Caulfield, B. P. (1986). Perception of neutral personality descriptions by depressed and nondepressed subjects. *Cognitive Therapy and Research, 10,* 31–36.

Vredenburg, K., Flett, G. L., & Krames, L. (1993). Analogue versus clinical depression: A critical reappraisal. *Psychological Bulletin, 113,* 327–344.

Wagenaar, W. A., Hudson, P. T. W., & Reason, J. T. (1990). Cognitive failures and accidents. *Applied Cognitive Psychology, 4,* 273–294.

Wagenaar, W. A., & Reason, J. T. (1990). Types and tokens in road accident causation. *Ergonomics, 33,* 1365–1375.

Wagner, H., & Manstead, A. (Eds.). (1989). *Handbook of social psychophysiology.* New York: Wiley.

Wallston, K. A. (1994). Cautious optimism vs. cockeyed optimism. *Psychology and Health, 9,* 201–203.

Warshaw, P. R., Calantone, R., & Joyce, M. (1986). A field application of the Fishbein and Ajzen intention model. *Journal of Social Psychology, 126,* 135–136.

Warshaw, P. R., & Davis, F. D. (1985). Disentangling behavioral intention and behavioral expectation. *Journal of Experimental Social Psychology, 21,* 213–228.

Wasserman, E. A. (1993). Comparative cognition: Beginning the second century of the study of animal intelligence. *Psychological Bulletin, 113,* 211–228.

Watson, J. B. (1913). Psychology as the behaviorist views it. *Psychological Review, 20,* 158–177.

Weinberg, R. S., Gould, D., Yukelson, D., & Jackson, A. (1981). The effect of pre-existing and manipulated self-efficacy on a competitive muscular endurance task. *Cognitive Therapy and Research, 4,* 345–354.

Weinstein, N. D. (1989). Optimistic biases about personal risks. *Science, 246,* 1232–1233.

Weinstein, N. D. (1993). Testing four competing theories of health–protective behavior. *Health Psychology, 12,* 324–333.

Weiskrantz, L. (1986). *Blindsight: A case study and implications.* Oxford, England: Oxford University Press.

Wilkins, W. (1986). Invalid evidence for expectancies as causes: Comment on Kirsch. *American Psychologist, 41,* 1387–1389.

Williams, S. L., Turner, S. M., & Peer, D. F. (1985). Guided mastery and performance desensitisation treatments for severe acrophobia. *Journal of Consulting and Clinical Psychology, 53,* 237–247.

Wilson, G. T. (1978). The importance of being theoretical: A commentary of Bandura's "Self-efficacy: Toward a unifying theory of behavioral change." *Advances in Behaviour Research and Therapy, 1,* 217–230.

Wilson, T. D. (1985). Strangers to ourselves: The origins and accuracy of beliefs about one's own mental status. In J. N. Harvey & G. Weary (Eds.), *Attribution: Basic issues and application* (pp. 9–36). New York: Academic Press.

Wilson, T. D., Dunn, D. S., Kraft, D., & Lisle, D. J. (1989). Introspection, attitude change, and attitude-behavior consistency: The disruptive effects of explaining why we feel the way we do. *Advances in Experimental Social Psychology, 22,* 287–343.

Wilson, T. D., Hodges, S. D., & LaFleur, S. J. (1995). Effects of introspecting about reasons: Inferring attitudes from accessible thoughts. *Journal of Personality and Social Psychology, 69,* 16–28.

Wilson, T. D., & LaFleur, S. J. (1995). Knowing what you'll do: Effects of analyzing reasons on self-prediction. *Journal of Personality and Social Psychology, 68,* 21–35.

Winett, R. A., & Winkler, R. C. (1972). Current behavior modifcation in the classroom: Be still, be quiet, be docile. *Journal of Applied Behavior Analysis, 5,* 499–504.

Winton, W. M., Putnam, I. E., & Krauss, R. M. (1984). Facial and autonomic manifestations of the dimensional structure of emotion. *Journal of Experimental Social Psychology, 20,* 195–216.

Wolpe, J. (1989). The derailment of behavior therapy: A tale of conceptual misdirection. *Journal of Behavior Therapy and Experimental Psychiatry, 20,* 3–15.

Wolpe, J. (1993). Commentary: The cognitivist oversell and comments on symposium contributions. *Journal of Behavior Therapy and Experimental Psychiatry, 24,* 141–147.

Wulfert, E., & Wan, C. K. (1993). Condom use: A self-efficacy model. *Health Psychology, 12,* 346–353.

Wurtele, S. K., & Maddux, J. E. (1987). Relative contributions of protection motivation theory components in predicting exercise intentions and behavior. *Health Psychology, 6,* 453–466.

Wyatt, W. J. (1990). Radical behaviorism misrepresented: A response to Mahoney. *American Psychologist, 45,* 1181–1183.

Xenakis, J. (1969). *Epictetus: Philosopher–therapist.* Den Haag: Martinus Nijhoff.

Zajonc, R. B. (1980). Feeling and thinking: Preferences need no inferences. *American Psychologist, 35,* 151–175.

Zajonc, R. B. (1984). On the primacy of affect. *American Psychologist, 39,* 117–123.

Zajonc, R. B., & Markus, H. (1984). Affect and cognition: The hard interface. In C. E. Izard, J. Kagan, & R. B. Zajonc (Eds.), *Emotion, cognition, and behaviour* (pp. 73–102). Cambridge, England: Cambridge University Press.

Zajonc, R. B., & Markus, H. (1985). Must all affect be mediated by cognition? *Journal of Consumer Research, 12,* 363–364.

Zajonc, R. B., Murphy, S. T., & Inglehart, M. (1989). Feeling and facial efference: Implications of the vascular theory of emotion. *Psychological Review, 96,* 395–416.

Zapf, D., & Reason, J. T. (1994). Introduction: Human errors and error handling. *Applied Psychology: An International Review, 43,* 431–432.

Author Index

Subject Index